A GUIDE TO
THE COTSWOLDS

A GUIDE TO THE COTSWOLDS

Richard Sale

The Crowood Press

First published in 1998 by
The Crowood Press Ltd
Ramsbury, Marlborough
Wiltshire SN8 2HR

British Library Cataloguing in Publication Data
A catalogue record for this book is available from the British Library.

ISBN 1 86126 101 2

Photograph on page 1: Minster Lovell.
Photograph previous page: Cecily Hill, Cirencester.

Typefaces used: Times New Roman (text); Franklin Gothic (captions and tables).

Typeset and designed by
D & N Publishing
Membury Business Park, Lambourn Woodlands
Hungerford, Berkshire.

Printed and bound by Paramount Printing Ltd,
Hong Kong

Contents

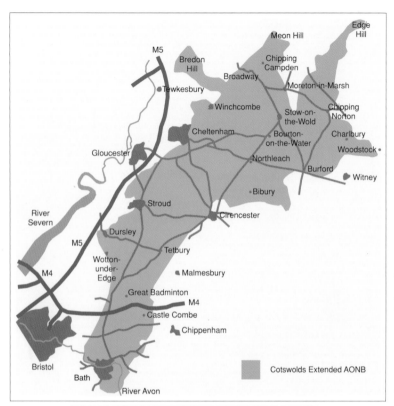

Key to Maps

———	Rivers	$\mathcal{A}$	Art/Crafts
▬▬▬	Motorways	$\mathcal{M}$	Museums
———	A Roads	🐂	Wildlife
———	B Roads	♣	Parks/Gardens
● ●	Minor roads	▣	Historical Buildings
● ·	Towns/villages	⊼	Archaeological site
P	Picnic sites	✳	Other

Introduction

There are few places as typically English as the Cotswolds. Here there are villages where cottages of golden stone are grouped around a green, while nearby stand a fine old manor house and an exquisite church, all with a story to tell. There are old castles and ruined abbeys. There are clear streams, fast-flowing through wonderful country, and viewpoints from where all these aspects of England can be seen. To spend time in the Cotswolds is to celebrate Englishness. Laurie Lee, whose sad death was reported while this book was being prepared, was born in the Cotswolds' Slad Valley, just to the north of Stroud. He famously noted that when he left the valley to travel to Spain he assumed that everywhere was just like Slad. He returned to live out his days in the valley because he had found that nowhere else was there anything to equal it.

This book explores the Cotswolds, visiting all the major towns, villages and places open to visitors in a series of tours. It seems a straightforward task, yet presents an immediate problem – how to define the Cotswolds. Ask anyone to write down a list of Cotswold villages and the list would start with the same places – Chipping Campden, Northleach, Bourton-on-the-Water, the Slaughters. But towards the end there would be varieties – just how far south do the Cotswolds extend?, how far east into Oxfordshire? To overcome the problem the definition used here is that area covered by the extended Cotswold Area of Outstanding Natural Beauty (AONB). This includes a finger of land extending to Edge Hill, and another which pushes eastwards as far as Woodstock. It also extends south as far as Bath. There will be those who maintain that to include Edge Hill and Blenheim Palace together with Broadway and Stanton is to stretch the Cotswold definition too far, but to use any other would be to invite criticism from others. The inclusion of the whole of the AONB allows some occasionally overlooked gems to be visited.

A Little Geology

The rocks underlying the Cotswolds were laid down while dinosaurs roamed the earth. The rock is a limestone, formed from sediments beneath a clear sea in which ammonites were numerous. It is an oolitic limestone, so-called – from the Greek oion lithos (egg stone) – because its sand-like granules, about 1,000 to each cubic centimetre, resemble compressed fish roe. This block of limestone was then tilted to create a characteristic escarpment/dip-slope. The escarpment (also known as a scarp slope and, here in the Cotswolds, frequently referred to as the Cotswold Edge) is steep and high, while the dip-slope is shallow and very long, sloping back from the scarp. The scarp slope forms a noticeable wall along the eastern edge of Severn Vale, reaching a height of almost 150m (500ft) in places. In general, the scarp is highest and steepest in the north, becoming less pronounced in the Southwolds and ending at the Avon Valley near Bath.

Most of the Cotswold rivers run down the scarp slope into the Severn, the rivers having eroded the limestone block to form a series of undulations that give the impression of hills. Indeed, even today some maps of the area name it (incorrectly) as Cotswold Hills. However, some rivers do flow eastwards, these include the Windrush, the Churn and the Leach, arguably the most beautiful of them all.

Cotswold limestone is a wonderful building material. When it is newly exposed to air it is soft enough to be sawn and carved easily, but on exposure a hard coating forms that resists water attack. It is also beautifully coloured, the colour ranging from golden, through pale honey to a delicate grey. The limestone also yielded a roofing tile. Close-grained rock was kept damp and covered until winter, when it was exposed to the air and well watered. Nightly drops in temperature froze the water in the cracks in the rock; this then split on thawing in exactly the way that central heating pipes are prone to do. The stone tiles produced were wonderfully weather-tight, but phenomenally heavy, requiring huge (and extremely expensive) oak beams to

Awkward Hill, Bibury.

support them. Though Cotswold stone-roofed houses are among the most attractive in the area, it is no surprise to discover that the thinner and much lighter tiles from the North Wales slate quarries rapidly killed the industry.

The stone is also used for the walling that is such a feature of the area. These walls, though, are much younger than most of the villages, having been built at the time of the Enclosure Acts when the great sheep wolds were taken for arable farming. The Cotswolds then become an area of green cereal fields defined by stone walls. Now, with yet more changes in farming styles, some of the old walls have gone and the Cotswold landscape in early summer is a patchwork of green and yellow, the yellow of oilseed rape.

A Little History

The earliest traces of man on the Cotswold landscape are the long barrows built by Neolithic folk. These are burial chambers – boxes formed of stone slab walls and roof – earthed over to form a long rectangle. The area's barrows are of a particular form implying that even at this early stage of man's occupation the Cotswolds were an important area. The people of the Bronze Age built round barrows over the cremated remains of

The King's Men, one of the Rollright Stone groups.

their dead. There are many of these in the Cotswolds, too, but they are less impressive than the long barrows and so are more often overlooked by the non-specialist. The other great legacy of the late Stone Age and the Bronze Age are the megaliths, huge stones arranged in circles or as enigmatic single stones. There is nothing to compare with Stonehenge, but at Great Rollright there are excellent examples of megalithic sites.

The Bronze Age ended when Iron Age folk reached Britain from Europe. They settled the Cotswolds, constructing many of their characteristic hillforts. At Birdlip, on the Cotswold Edge, an excavated horde of Iron Age jewellery included a bronze mirror, one of the finest pieces to have been discovered to date from the period. From AD43 Iron Age Celts were absorbed into the Roman empire. For the Romans the Cotswolds were also important, forming an early western border to their new colony and later being traversed by several of their most important roads. Fosse Way, Akeman Street and Ermin Way not only crossed the area, but met at Corinium, Roman Britain's most important town after London. Today Corinium is Cirencester, but the town's Roman past is remembered in the Corinium Museum, one of the best Roman museums (and one of the finest museums of any type) in the country. Close to Cirencester, there are other important Roman remains, particularly Chedworth Villa, while at Bath there are the most complete Roman baths discovered in Britain to date.

Soon after the Romans left Britain Saxons from continental Europe began their westward expansion across the country. Their advance was halted by King Arthur at Badon (on the

Ridgeway?), but when it began again one of the most significant battles was fought at Hinton Hill near Dyrham. The Saxon victory here isolated the Celts of the West Country from those of Wales, making Saxon control of England much easier. The Saxons have left fewer remains than the Romans (though the churches of the Duntisbourne Valley are a notable exception) but they did give the area many of its place names. In particular, a chieftain called Cod gave his name to a section of the high plateau (the wold) near the source of the River Windrush. Cod's wold has now become the name for the entire plateau. It should be noted, though, that some, but less romantic, experts believe that cod could also derive from cote, a hollow, or cot, an animal enclosure.

When the Normans invaded they too recognized the importance of the area. For a time Gloucester was England's capital and the Normans brought the sheep that were to make the Cotswolds the most prosperous area in Britain and one of the most important in Europe. Some experts claim that the sheep, a heavy-fleeced animal which became known as the Cotswold lion, was introduced by the Romans, but most believe it unlikely that the breed could have survived the Dark Ages. Later, when the

The Saxon church at Duntisbourne Rouse.

woollen industry went into decline, the sheep almost died out. It was saved by a group of enthusiasts who formed the Cotswold Sheep Society at the end of the nineteenth century, and the breed may now be seen in one or two places in the area, most notably at the Cotswold Farm Park on the high wolds near Temple Guiting. The importance of the wool trade can be seen from the fact that the British Lord Chancellor still sits on a woolsack in the House of Lords chamber. Woolsacks also adorn the tops of tombs in churchyards shaded by 'wool churches', buildings paid for by the rich wool merchants. These merchants also built themselves wonderful houses, many still the centres of attraction in Cotswold towns and villages. Around the great houses were the cottages of the wool trade workers, the buildings on which the allure of the Cotswolds' villages is built. At the height of the trade it is estimated that there were over half a million sheep on the wolds, and over half the area's inhabitants earned a living from them. At first much of the wool was exported to Europe to be made into cloth, but it was soon realized that the exports made no economic sense. The merchants then brought European weavers to the Cotswolds to teach the techniques to their workers. Soon Cotswold woollen cloth was the equal of its European counterpart and the merchants grew even richer.

When, following the Civil War, the wool trade declined sharply the effect on the workers was devastating. The government tried to halt the decline, one of the more desperate measures being the Burial in Woollen Act of 1678 which decreed that all shrouds had to be made of wool. As with all the other measures tried, this did not work. The decline accelerated, hunger riots breaking out in several towns. The migration of the workers from the villages in search of work led to the villages being 'time-capsuled', there being no building nor development for several centuries. It is surely ironic that the suffering of the Cotswold folk and the 'deaths' of their villages has made the area such a wonderful place for today's visitors.

(Opposite) The Old Fountain, Dumbleton.

Cheltenham and the North-Western Cotswolds

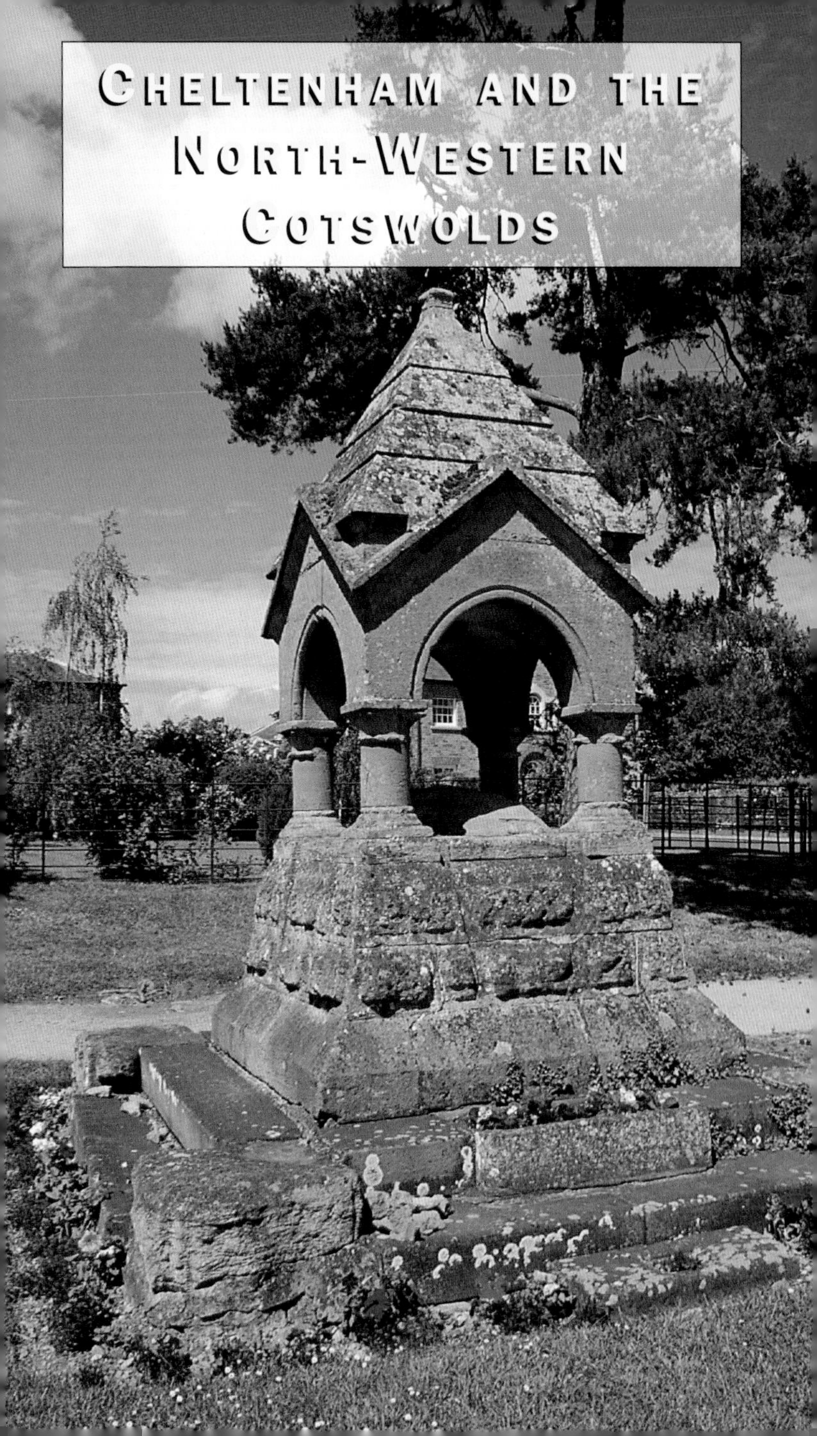

Cheltenham

Cheltenham, the self-styled 'Centre for the Cotswolds' (no bad description, despite the town's position on the area's eastern edge) is an elegant, gracious place. As with England's other great spa towns, the elegance is recent, a stark contrast to Cheltenham's early years when it was an undistinguished village nestling below the Cotswold scarp edge. The granting of a market charter in 1226 had raised the village's status, but it was not until 1716 that the discovery was made which dramatically improved its fortunes.

William Mason, a hosier in fledgling Cheltenham, had bought a field at Bayshill in 1704 with the intention of farming it, but he had done little by 1716. In that year he noticed that pigeons were persistently pecking near a trickle of water running at the edge of the field. On investigating he found that the birds were pecking at crystals beside the stream. Cheltenham was close enough to Bath for Mason to become excited: he had an analysis carried out and the results showed a pure mineral water. Mason therefore dug to find the mineral spring, but discovered it to be in the next field. He therefore bought that field, uncovered the spring and erected a wooden shelter over it. Then he stopped. Bath's fame rested on the ability of visitors to bathe in its water. Mason's trickle barely amounted to enough to fill a washbasin.

William Mason's daughter Elizabeth was married to a retired sea captain, Henry Skillicorne, a man whose past seems to have been murky, perhaps even including small-scale piracy. Certainly he had a ready eye for business, and when Elizabeth inherited the Bayshill site on her father's death, Henry set about turning it into money-making spa. True there was not enough water for bathing, but there was enough to drink.

In 1739 Skillicorne planted avenues of lime and elm trees, creating the Upper and Lower Walks. He erected a picturesque bridge over the River Chelt. In 1740 a Dr Short published his findings on the water, claiming that it was superior to any other in the country. Business improved and Henry built a brick

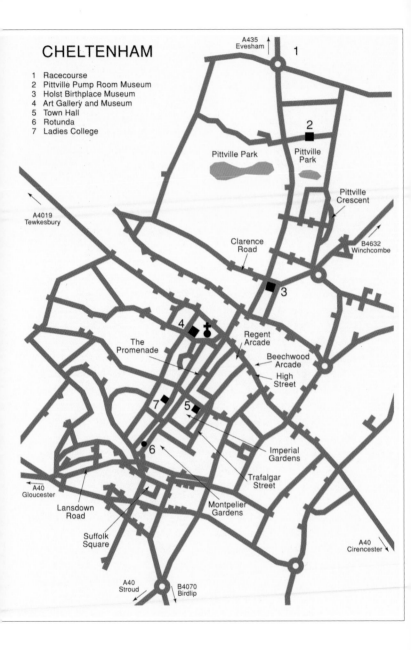

CHELTENHAM

1 Racecourse
2 Pittville Pump Room Museum
3 Holst Birthplace Museum
4 Art Gallery and Museum
5 Town Hall
6 Rotunda
7 Ladies College

A435
Evesham

1

2

Pittville Park

Pittville
Park

Pittville
Crescent

A4019
Tewkesbury

B4632
Winchcombe

Clarence
Road

3

4

Regent
Arcade

The
Promenade

Beechwood
Arcade

High
Street

7

5

Imperial
Gardens

6

Trafalgar
Street

A40
Gloucester

Lansdown
Road

Montpelier
Gardens

Suffolk
Square

A40
Cirencester

A40
Stroud

B4070
Birdlip

wellhouse to cover his asset. As a tribute to the pigeons who had 'discovered' the spring, a stone pigeon sat on each of the house's corners. Today a pigeon still sits on top of Cheltenham's crest.

In 1963 a statue of Skillicorne was erected behind the Town Hall to mark the bicentenary of his death. Henry's son William improved the facilities, even adding limited bathing, but Cheltenham seemed destined to remain a second-class spa. Then, in 1788, Lord Fauconberg, who had invested money in the Skillicorne holdings, persuaded King George III, Queen Charlotte and the three princesses to spend five weeks at Cheltenham. Fanny Burney, one of the Queen's ladies-in-waiting was not impressed. The walks were 'clay and sided by common trees without any rich foliage'. Bayshill House, in which they stayed, was small, her own room had just space to crowd in a bed, a chest of drawers and three small chairs. As for the Queen – 'she is obliged to dress and undress (in her drawing room), for she has no toilet apartment!' To cap it all, Fanny was required to drink her tea in a corridor.

But the King enjoyed the visit, and despite the fact that within a few weeks of leaving Cheltenham he was to have the first attack of the illness which was to plague the rest of his life ('madness' stemming from the metabolic disorder porphyria), the reputation of Cheltenham and its waters was secured. Wellington came to see whether the waters could cure his liver problems and recommended them to his officers. Visitors increased and building work accelerated. The legacy of that building is the finest Regency town in England.

Later, here at Cheltenham as elsewhere, taking the waters ceased to be part of the social round. There was a decrease in building and a dip in prosperity, but the decline also prevented wholesale redevelopment, so that the Regency terraces were preserved. Today Cheltenham is prosperous again, as a walk along any of its central shopping streets will quickly confirm. The town's motto is 'pretty, poor and proud'. Pretty certainly; proud – rightly so; but it is a long time since poor would have been a useful adjective for anyone describing it.

To savour the best of the town, start at the southern end, where the 'village' of Leckhampton merges with Cheltenham. A good introduction to the finest architecture is Suffolk Square, a quiet part of the town, tucked away from the main shopping areas. The Square was designed by Edward Jenkins, a little-known local architect, and is still a model of simple elegance. The nearby area around Suffolk Parade and Suffolk Road has the best of Cheltenham's antique shops and some of its best restaurants. Visitors to the antiques shops will need to spend hard to compete with Ronald Summerfield, a Cheltenham man whose collection had risen to over one million items when he died in 1989. Some of the items Summerfield left to the Town Museum; what remained was sold at an auction of over 14,000 lots lasting 25 days, the biggest single collection auction ever held in Britain and which raised £8 million for Summerfield's estate.

Close to Suffolk Square are Montpellier Gardens. These and the Imperial Gardens to the north are well-tended and colourful, confirming the town's status as a winner of the 'Britain in Bloom' competition. The Gardens are home to a superb bandstand, beautifully restored by the Civic Society, where military bands once entertained spa visitors. They are also home to one of only two statues of William IV in the country (erected in 1833, apparently to celebrate the passing of the Reform Bill, which must be almost as rare a commemoration as is the subject), and what must surely be the finest tennis-court booking office in Britain. On the southern edge of the Gardens is Montpellier Terrace, one of the elegant rows of terraced houses erected by John Papworth who, together with the Jearrad Brothers, was largely responsible for Regency Cheltenham. Interestingly, John Papworth's middle name was Buonarotti (Michelangelo's surname), a remarkable piece of prescience on the part of his parents. To Papworth we owe the wide streets which enhance the terraces. At No. 91 a plaque remembers Dr Edward Wilson, a member of Captain Scott's ill-fated expedition to the South Pole, who was born there. At the end of the Terrace the Lansdown area of the town, with more Regency houses, lies to the left. The gently curving Lansdown Crescent, with its colonnaded entrances, is particularly good, but pride of place must go to Papworth's Tivoli Road, with its array of beautiful individual (rather than terraced) houses, set behind equally beautiful trees. Sir Ralph Richardson, the actor, was born at No. 11. Ahead is the Montpellier Spa building, now occupied by Lloyd's Bank. Here there was a ballroom-cum-concert hall: Gustav Holst's *Scherzo and Intermezzo* had its first performance at the Spa. The Rotunda was added to the Spa in 1826, Papworth having been inspired by the Pantheon in Rome. Inside, the dome is beautifully decorated and there is a magnificent eighteenth-century Italian marble fountain.

Papworth maintained the classical allusion with Montpellier Walk, beside the Spa, the shops being separated by Caryatids in a clear reference to the Erechtheion, on the Acropolis at Athens. One of shops (close to the Rotunda) is O'Neills, a link between Cheltenham's spa town history and one of its main modern attractions, the National Hunt Festival.

Follow Montpellier Walk north towards the town centre. Running parallel to it and reached by a small arcade is Montpellier Street, the elegant shops on its western side set beyond a wide pavement, itself at the top of steps from the road. The Courtyard, a small, galleried group of shops, is a more recent development, its design being harmonized with the older architecture. Beyond Montpellier Walk is the Promenade, often claimed to be the most beautiful street in Britain. At its southern end the Promenade has one of the town's most elegant Regency terraces. Especially good is the ironwork. In an age of steel it is easy to forget that in

A Caryatid, Montpellier Walk, Cheltenham.

18

Regency times wrought iron was the new material and the height of fashion. There are good examples elsewhere – a porch in Montpellier Terrace is a remarkable example, and there are exquisite canopied balconies in London Road on the eastern edge of Regency Cheltenham – but this terrace is a particular favourite. Across from the terrace the Imperial Gardens are another colourful open space at the heart of the town. In summer, open-air art exhibitions are held at its northern edge, close to the Town Hall. The baroque Town Hall, built in 1902, is one of the main centres for two of Cheltenham's four famous festivals, those of Music and Literature. At the opposite end of the Gardens is the Queen's Hotel, built in 1878 on the site of the Imperial Spa. Queen's was to have been called King's, but William IV died before it was opened. The Hotel, the work of Robert and Charles Jearrad, has been host to guests as diverse as Prince Louis Jerome Napoleon and Bob Hope.

The Promenade continues into the town, but mirrors itself beyond the road junction, a row of quality shops lining the right side, with a neat garden on the left, in front of the imposing terrace (Regency with classical overtones) which now houses, among other things, the town's Tourist Information Office.

Imperial Gardens, Cheltenham.

19

In the little garden fronting the terrace is the town's cenotaph and a statue of Edward Wilson, gazing east rather than south, but clad for the epic journey. The statue was created in 1914 by Scott's widow. Nearby is a Neptune fountain inspired, it is said by Rome's Trevi Fountain. The plaque at its back notes its construction from Portland Stone (in the Cotswolds!) and that it was designed by a committee, which seems no surprise. A recent attempt to refurbish Neptune by replacing the arm and trident lost some time ago was thwarted by a senseless act of vandalism, the hand being broken on the night of the restoration in an attempt to remove the trident.

To the west of the Promenade lies Cheltenham Ladies' College. Cheltenham College, a public school for boys, was founded in 1841. Its delightful buildings, in large part in Gothic style, stand beside Bath Road, the road to Leckhampton. It is in the grounds of the College that Cheltenham's Cricket Festival (the third of the four famous festivals) is held. Cheltenham has a place in cricketing history as the only ground to date where a hat-trick of stumpings has taken place (Gloucestershire vs Somerset, 1893). Cecil Day Lewis the poet was once a master at the College. The Ladies' College was founded later, in 1853, when a group of men which included the Principal of the (Boys) College decided that there should be an equivalent for the 'daughters of Noblemen and Gentlemen'. The Ladies' College stands on the site of the Royal Well, where George III took the waters. The College buildings are imposing rather than beautiful, but do include the curious onion-dome which can be seen peeping over the Promenade's Regency terrace when it is viewed from the Imperial Gardens. Dorothea Beale, one of the greatest names in the education of girls was made Principal of the College in 1858 at the age of 27 and remained in post until her death in 1906.

To the east of the Promenade, beyond Imperial Gardens, is Trafalgar Street, named in honour of a former resident, Captain Hardy, who held the dying Nelson on HMS *Victory*. Also to the east is Cheltenham's main shopping area. In Regent Street is the Everyman Theatre (opened in October 1891 with a performance

The Wishing Fish Clock, Regent Arcade, Cheltenham.

starring Lily Langtry) and the entrance to the Regent Arcade, one of the town's premier shopping areas, opened in 1985. On its lower floor the Arcade houses the Wishing Fish Clock. The clock, installed in 1987, was designed by Kit Williams who wrote and illustrated *Masquerade* while living in Horsley, near Stroud. The book, with its hidden treasure hunt theme, caused a sensation at the time, as did the Clock. It is claimed to be the tallest in the world (at 14m – 45ft – and weighing 3 tonnes), and with its rolling balls, mice and huge, bubble-blowing fish, always attracts crowds on the hour. At the other end of the Arcade is the High Street, a continuation of the shopping centre. From it the Beechwood Arcade leads off. Though smaller than the Regent Arcade, this miniature American shopping mall with its central water garden is also very popular.

Behind the Municipal Offices is Royal Crescent. It is no surprise to discover that this early terrace (built in 1805) was the work of a Bath architect. The Crescent is superb, but sadly spoilt by having the town's bus station immediately in front of it. Close to the Crescent is the Town Museum and Art Gallery, housed in a building nearing its centenary and topped by a tower that is another of Cheltenham's architectural curios. The Museum has excellent sections on the history of the town and of the Cotswolds, and one devoted to the life and work of Edward Wilson. The Gallery section includes one of the most important collections of work by followers of William Morris, the poet and designer. The collection includes jewellery, stained glass and furniture. The Museum has a continuous programme of temporary exhibitions.

Behind the Museum is St. Mary's, Cheltenham's parish church. The church, built in the twelfth century, but with additions and alterations throughout its subsequent history, is most notable for its windows, including a superb rose window, and the memorial to Henry Skillicorne. His epitaph on the memorial is a history of the development of Cheltenham and, at 587 words and the longest in Britain, is a far from potted history. The path on the south side of the church has brass measuring marks for cloth set in it; look, too, for the delightful lampstandards and the gravestone of John Higgs, a pig slaughterer who died in 1825. The humour shown on the stone is as sharp a contrast to the norm as Higgs's knife obviously was.

Close to the church is the Roman Catholic Priory Church of St. Gregory the Great, built in the mid-nineteenth century despite its Gothic lines. The tall elegant spire is one of most distinctive sights in the town. Cheltenham has many other good churches, too many to deal with individually, but try to spare time for a look at Christ Church in Lansdown, whose tower dominates the area.

To the north of the High Street, on the way to Prestbury, is Clarence Street, where No. 4 is a museum to Gustav Holst who was born there on 21 September 1874 (though at that time the street was known as Pittville Terrace). Holst was the son of the music teacher at Cheltenham Grammar School, who was also the organist at All Saints' Church. Not surprisingly Gustav was interested in music from an early age: by the time he was four he was already showing signs of a prodigious talent. He played the violin, piano and trombone, and sang in the choir, and by the time he was 16 (and a pupil at the Grammar School) was already having his own music performed. At 17 he was organist and choirmaster at St. Lawrence's Church in Wyck Rissington, though this position lasted only a year as he enrolled at the Royal College of Music in London when he was 18. From that time on Holst's life was spent away from Cheltenham, but he returned in 1927 to conduct the Bournemouth Symphony Orchestra in his suite *The Planets* at the Town Hall. He claimed that this was one of the more memorable moments of his life. The Museum has his grand piano and a collection of memorabilia in rooms decorated in Regency and Victorian styles. The plaque to the composer, who died in 1934, was unveiled by his friend and fellow composer Vaughan Williams in 1949.

Perhaps this is a suitable moment to mention another musical son of Cheltenham, though one whose musical and life styles could hardly have been more different. Brian Jones was born in the town in 1942, achieving fame as a guitarist with the Rolling Stones. His influence on the band was significant, but fame and what went with it – the intensity of work and travel, and drugs – affected his health. In 1969 he left the band and drowned, in still mysterious circumstances, just a few weeks later. He is buried in the Priors Road cemetery, his grave a shrine to fans of the band's early music.

North of the Holst Museum is Pittville. Joseph Pitt was born in Little Witcombe in 1759 and, legend has it, was holding gentleman's horses for a penny when a Cirencester solicitor recognized that he was a bright boy and took him on as an office junior. Pitt was indeed bright and became a self-taught solicitor of such cleverness that he rapidly had his own successful company. He invested his money, in part, in land to the north of Cheltenham. By 1820 Pitt had 100 acres of land and began his great project – the creation of Pittville, a new town which, he hoped, would bring him even greater wealth. Pittville's focus was to be a new Pump Room. This was completed in 1830, the work of John Forbes: it is a magnificent building, its Ionic columns and design being based on the Temple of Illisus in Athens. It has an oval pump room, a ballroom, library and billiard rooms, and the first floor has a balcony from which visitors could watch the activities below. Today the Pump Rooms host events at the Music and Literature Festivals. It is worth visiting for its Regency splendour; visitors may still take the waters. The Pump Rooms also house a museum of Cheltenham's history from Regency to modern times. The collections include original costumes, dating from the mid-eighteenth to the twentieth century, and the jewellery that would have been popular with those who wore the dresses.

Pittville Pump Rooms, Cheltenham.

The Pump Rooms were (and still are) set in an expansive park where a stream was dammed to create a lake. Today the lake's ducks and swans pursue strollers for a share of their sandwiches, while children enjoy the little playground. Around the park Pitt planned 600 houses in a complex of terraces and crescents. But by 1824 Cheltenham's housing development had slowed to a stop, and by the following year the bottom had fallen out of the market. Pitt was ruined. At his death in 1842 he was still in debt, what remained of his estate being sold to pay off his creditors. Of Pitt's planned new town only the buildings of Clarence Square, Pittville Lawn and Wellington Square were completed. Pitt's name lives on though, the entire area still being called Pittville, and Pittville Circus (completed just before his death on land he had been forced to sell) has been renamed, having originally been Albert Circus in honour of Prince Albert.

Beyond Pittville is Cheltenham's racecourse, the setting for the fourth of the town's famous festivals. Horseracing was part of the social scene from the Spa's early days, though it was not until 1831 that the first races were held on Prestbury Park, the site of the present course. Even then the Park was not a permanent home until 1901, grandstands on several other sites also being used. The present vast grandstand was opened by Queen Elizabeth, the Queen Mother, in 1979. The March festival of racing under National Hunt rules is Britain's foremost steeplechase meeting, its most famous races being the Champion Hurdle and the Gold Cup. The history of the course, and of steeplechasing in Britain, is explored at the Hall of Fame at the course. Here visitors can reflect on the achievements of Golden Miller (who won five successive Gold Cups), Arkle (who won three Gold Cups from three starts) and other famous horses and riders. It is perhaps fitting that one of horseracing's greatest jockeys, Fred Archer, should have been Cheltenham-born, in a cottage by St. George's Place in 1857. Archer's life was a tragedy – he was tall for a jockey, the endless diets and purges needed to bring him to racing weight destroying his health and leading to his suicide at the age of 29 – but his career was one of the greatest the sport has seen.

ADDRESSES AND OPENING TIMES

TOWN MUSEUM AND ART GALLERY,
Clarence Street *(01242 237431)*
❖
OPEN: all year, Mon–Sat, 10.00am–5.20pm,
closed Bank Holidays

CHELTENHAM COLLEGE,
Bath Road *(01242 513540)*
❖
OPEN: by request at the Bursar's Office

HALL OF FAME, Cheltenham Racecourse,
Prestbury Park *(01242 513014)*
❖
OPEN: all year, Mon–Fri, 9.30am–4.30pm

HOLST BIRTHPLACE MUSEUM,
4 Clarence Road *(01242 524846)*
❖
OPEN: all year, Tues–Sat, 10.00am–4.20pm,
closed Bank Holidays

PITTVILLE PUMP ROOM/PUMP ROOM MUSEUM,
Albert Road *(01242 523852)*
❖
OPEN: May–Sept, daily except Tues, 10.00am–4.30pm;
Oct–April, daily except Tues, 11.00am–4.00pm

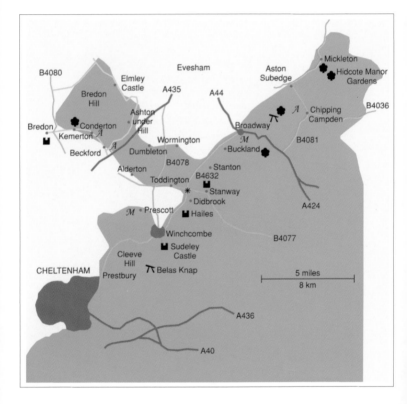

TOUR 1: Cheltenham and the Spring Line Villages

Our first tour explores the villages that lie on the spring line below the Cotswold Edge (the scarp slope), finishing at Chipping Campden where the Edge turns east above the Vale of Evesham.

Leaving Cheltenham the first place passed is Prestbury, now officially part of the town, but once a village in its own right. Indeed, before the discovery of the mineral springs, Prestbury was the more important of the two villages, its importance being based on its market; The Burgage (the old Market Place) is the most impressive street. It was at Prestbury, where his father was landlord of the King's Arms, that Fred Archer, the famous jockey, spent his childhood. Despite his tragic death, Archer is not one of the ghosts reputed to haunt a village which claims to be the most haunted in Britain.

Beyond Prestbury the B4632 climbs steeply up the flank of Cleeve Hill. Towards the top there are parking places for those wishing to explore the hill. The highest point of the Cotswolds, on Cleeve Common, a short distance to the east of **Cleeve Hill**, may also be reached by road from Charlton Kings or Whittington. It stands at 330m (1,082ft), though the actual summit – marked by an Ordnance Survey triangulation point next to a wall and the transmission masts, both of which are taller – is undistinguished. The oolitic limestone of the Cotswolds is packed with bivalve fossils and the rock outcrops on the hill are a good place to find them. The largest of the outcrops, Cleeve Cloud, is also used by local rock

Radio masts, triangulation point and panorama dial on the edge of Cleeve Hill.

climbers, though the fragile nature of the rock means that it is unlikely ever to be a popular venue. The outcrop's name derives from the Old English for a cliff – cliff clud, cliff of rock.

Cleeve Hill is visited by the Cotswold Way, the excellent long-distance footpath that explores the Cotswold Edge, so that those who walk up the hill from the B4632 are likely to meet walkers crossing the high plateau. The objective for both is the panorama dial which points out the highlights of the superb view. Anciently a part of the hill was enclosed, probably during the Iron Age. To the natural defensive barrier of the cliff, a double rampart and ditch were added to create a hillfort enclosing about two acres of hilltop. It is thought that double rather than single ditches were needed to cope with the newly-discovered slingshot. Today golf balls have replaced stones as missiles, some of the ditches protecting the greens of the hill's course.

Cleeve is also the site of The Ring, a poorly understood circular bank and ditch about 25m (30yd) across. It is conjectured that the structure predates the hillfort and may even be an early form of henge site – a stone circle without the stones. Another, and much better understood, ancient site is reached by turning off the B4632 towards the bottom of Cleeve Hill (continuing along the road past the parking places). Just after passing Postlip (to the right, where there is a fine Jacobean manor house in the grounds of which stands a Norman church) turn right along the narrow lane signed for **Belas Knap**, climbing steeply.

Belas Knap is a long barrow, a burial chamber from the Neolithic (New Stone) Age, and is probably about 4,000 years old. In its simplest form a long barrow was a 'box' of stone slabs covered with a rectangular mound of earth. From many such sites the earth has disappeared, blown away over the centuries to leave the slabs exposed as a dolmen or cromlech. At Belas Knap the mound remains, creating the distinctive long-barrow shape. However, Belas Knap is not from the first phase of barrow construction. In its earliest form the burial chamber was approached direct from the outside: there would have been a closing slab and, usually, 'horns' where the barrow

The 'false portal', Belas Knap.

extended to create an entranceway, perhaps where rituals were performed during the burial. Possibly to prevent tomb robbing, or perhaps in an effort to confuse evil spirits, the barrow builders began to construct 'false portals', as here at Belas Knap where the elaborate drystone-walled horns lead to a blind entrance, the burial chambers being reached from the sides of the mound. There are four chambers from which the remains of thirty-one people have been excavated. The chambers can be entered, though nothing now remains. Belas Knap is in the care of English Heritage and may be visited at any time.

Close to Belas Knap are the remains of a later site, the Roman villa at Wadfield. This, of which little more than a section of mosaic floor remains, lies on private land and may only be visited with permission.

At the bottom of B4632 as it descends from Cleeve Hill lies **Winchcombe**. For those new to the Cotswolds, arriving from the splendours of Regency Cheltenham, Winchcombe is a marvellous introduction. Not as pretty as some of the spring line and wold villages to the north and the east, but a great deal less of a tourist honeypot than some more famous places, its array of Cotswold houses – warm stone, Cotswold tiles and neat gables – being as good as any. It is a straggling village, but the most delightful area from the Corner Cupboard Inn, past the church to the High Street is compact enough to be covered in an easy stroll.

Belas Knap and Wadfield Roman villa suggest a long history, but the town's recorded history starts in Saxon times when Kenulf, who became king of Mercia shortly after the death of the famous King Offa in 796, founded an abbey here. Kenulf died in 819 and was succeeded by his son Kenelm. Kenelm was only a boy and had a scheming older sister Quendreda who coveted her brother's throne. Quendreda persuaded her lover Ascobert, Kenelm's tutor, to murder the boy. Ascobert did kill him, one version of the legend having it that Kenelm woke from an afternoon nap to find Ascobert digging a grave. The boy told Ascobert it was in the wrong place and led him to the correct one, identified by the miraculous blooming of an ash twig. Ascobert was clearly not a man to be put off by miracles and chopped Kenelm's head off. A dove emerged from the boy's head with a scroll in its beak and flew tirelessly to Rome where it laid the scroll at the Pope's feet. The scroll indicated the position of the body and the monks of Winchcombe Abbey were sent to retrieve it. The body was brought back to Winchcombe where Kenelm was laid beside his father, the knife that Ascobert had used being buried with the boy. Interestingly, during excavations of the Abbey site in 1815 two coffins were discovered, one containing the body of a man, the other that of a boy and a long knife.

As is usually the case with such stories, there were miracles along the route taken by the monks as they brought Kenelm's body back to Winchcombe. The most significant were the gushing of a spring at a resting point near what is now the site of Sudeley Castle, and the blinding of Quendreda. The spring, St. Kenelm's well, is marked by a nineteenth-century reconstruction of the original well (continue past Sudeley Castle on the road towards Guiting Power: the well is to the left about 700m [half a mile] beyond the castle entrance). Quendreda was in the Mercian king's palace at Winchcombe (on the site now occupied by Lloyds Bank in Abbey Terrace) when the monks carried Kenelm's body past. Hearing the noise, she looked out at the procession and, on seeing the coffin, her eyes promptly fell from their sockets. To expunge her guilt Quendreda became Abbess of Southminster.

Kenelm's miraculous remains brought Winchcombe great wealth and prestige, the Abbey being a major pilgrimage site for centuries, though the prosperity the pilgrims brought the towns-folk did not lead to completely harmonious relations between them and the monks. For over 150 years, from the mid-thirteenth century, there was an on-off feud between the two groups, usually involving the ringing of church bells (the townsfolk had their own church) at ungodly hours, but sometimes involving brawls. Only in 1399 was the feuding brought to a conclusion by a Papal decree on the acceptable times for bell ringing.

Winchcombe Abbey was dissolved by Henry VIII two days before Christmas 1539. The site was granted to the Seymours of nearby Sudeley Castle who ransacked it. The townspeople then stole what remained – the building stone (persistent visitors will find stones marked with a 'W' in houses close to Abbey Terrace, in Court Lane, for instance) – so that now nothing at all remains; a cross marks the position of the high altar on the private land behind the high wall on Abbey Terrace's northern side.

The destruction of the Abbey all but destroyed Winch-combe, and the fleeting prosperity it derived from the growing of tobacco was also ended when the government banned its production in order to safeguard the livelihood of the new American colonies. The locals did not take kindly to the ban and there were riots when cavalry was sent in to destroy the crop. The production did leave one oddity, the presence of a Tobacco Close in Winchcombe, to the occasional bemusement of visitors. Another street, Silk Mill Lane, commemorates a later attempt to restore Winchcombe's prosperity.

Today the town is quietly prosperous, with a couple of inns worth considering for lunch, and a church famous for its gargoyles. The George Inn, in the High Street, was rebuilt in the early sixteenth century by Richard Kidderminster, the most famous of Abbot of Winchcombe. Richard chose to rebuild rather than refurbish an existing inn (called 'Le George' and with Norman origins) when he wanted a lodging place for scholars studying at the Abbey. The initials RK may still be seen above the entrance to the courtyard. A local legend has it that a Royalist soldier was discovered at the inn when the plume from his hat fell from the gallery (now one of the George's most endearing parts). The Royalist was probably less enamoured of the gallery when he was taken outside and shot.

Opposite the George is the Town Hall. The town stocks in front of it (neatly roofed to keep offenders dry while the townsfolk hurled rotten fruit at them, a somewhat curiously thoughtful gesture) are in keeping with the small museum inside, which has a collection of police uniforms and equipment from all over the world, together with another on the history of the town.

The sixteenth-century Corner Cupboard Inn lies close to the B4632's entry into the town, a delightful building in purest Cotswold style. Close to it is a railway museum, run by enthusiasts, with an amazing collection of memorabilia including a signal box and booking office.

Between the inns is St. Peter's Church, built in about 1470 in Perpendicular style. The tower still shows the marks of Roundhead shot from a Civil War skirmish, the holes at the tower's base being from bullets when a group of Royalist prisoners were lined up and shot. The tower is topped by one of the Cotswolds' finest weathercocks, a bird which once graced the spire of St. Mary Redcliffe in Bristol. Also on the outside are a group of remarkable gargoyles. They are known locally as Winchcombe Worthies from a story that they are caricatures of local dignitaries, though that cannot satisfactorily explain the demons. Some have suggested that they were intended to frighten off evil spirits that were attempting to enter the church along with the

The Corner Cupboard Inn, Winchcombe.

congregation. Perhaps they were just the stonemasons exercising their craft and imagination and having a little fun.

Inside the church are the stone coffins which may have held Kenulf and Kenelm; an almsbox carved from a single tree, with three locks to obey Edward IV's edict that such boxes could be opened only in the presence of the vicar and both churchwardens; a fourteenth-century altar cloth made from a pair of priest's copes, one of which, with the pomegranate emblem, may have been made by Catherine of Aragon; and an organ case that some have suggested is the work of Grinling Gibbons. The memorial to Sir Thomas Williams is poignant: he is shown kneeling beside his tomb staring across at a recess that was to have been filled by a statue of his wife. She married again and is buried with her second husband, leaving poor Sir Thomas to kneel alone.

Opposite the church are the Jacobean House, built in 1619 as a school, and possibly the work of Inigo Jones, and the late sixteenth century Chandos Almshouses. Nearby is Vineyard Street (formerly Duck Street, as the plaque notes, when it led to a stream where 'scolds' were ducked in a ducking stool). Follow the street to reach **Sudeley Castle**.

The first castle at Sudeley was built in the twelfth century, but the site's history really begins with Ralph Boteler in the fifteenth. Boteler fought in France with Henry V and Henry VI, and was present when Joan of Arc was burnt at the stake. It was he who built what largely remains today. The Portmore Tower was named for a French admiral taken prisoner by Boteler during one of Henry V's campaigns and ransomed for a sum sufficient to complete the castle. When finished, Sudeley aroused considerable envy because of its beautiful lines and position. When Boteler was captured during the Wars of the Roses the story is told that he took one last look and said 'Sudeley, it is you that art the traitor, not I.' In reality Boteler had merely chosen the wrong side.

Ultimately the castle was granted by Edward VI to Thomas Seymour, his uncle and the brother of the Lord Protector. Seymour was an ambitious man and Sudeley played a central role in the machinations that followed the reign of Henry VIII. Henry had already stayed at Sudeley with Anne Boleyn; Thomas Seymour was the brother of Jane Seymour, Edward VI's mother, and married Henry's widow Katherine Parr; both Henry's daughters, Mary and Elizabeth, each a future Queen, spent time at the castle; and Lady Jane Grey, Seymour's niece, left from here on her ill-fated bid to secure the crown. It is has been claimed that Thomas Seymour attempted to seduce Princess Elizabeth here when she was fifteen, and, even more sensationally, that Elizabeth died at Sudeley and was replaced with a local boy by the ever-artful Seymour. The legend doubtless grew up to explain the Queen's decision never to marry and her distinctly 'manly' manner of conducting Crown affairs.

Ultimately Thomas lost his head for his scheming (as part of the plot that also saw the execution of Lady Jane Grey and her husband). That was after Katherine Parr's death, shortly after giving birth to his only child, a daughter. Seymour longed for a son, his disappointment was profound and history records nothing more of the girl after his execution.

During the Civil War, Sudeley was a Royalist stronghold at first – indeed, it was at one time the King's headquarters – but fell to the Roundheads in 1643. The Puritan soldiers treated it in appalling fashion, half demolishing parts to prevent its further use as a castle, desecrating the chapel and generally creating havoc. When the war ended Sudeley was abandoned, decaying still further. One curious footnote is the accidental discovery, in 1782, of Katherine Parr's lead coffin. The farmer who found it opened it and found the Queen's body completely preserved. The coffin seems to have been opened several times subsequently, but was eventually reburied in 1817. The castle then became the property of the Dent family. They restored, or, at least, stabilized much of the fabric and raised a marble tomb over Queen Katherine's remains.

Today Sudeley is a magnificent place, set in gardens and parkland that are equally good. The evocative ruins of the Banqueting Hall stand beside the Portmore Tower and the more

Sudeley Castle gardens.

(Left) Katherine Parr's Tomb, Sudeley Castle.

complete castle structures, the latter housing an exhibition on Sudeley's place in Tudor history and a collection of other historical treasures and art works. The historical items include Cromwell's beer mug, while the art includes work by Van Dyck, Rubens, Constable and Tanner. The complete rooms include the nursery created for the daughter of Thomas Seymour and Katherine Parr.

Katherine Parr's tomb is found in St. Mary's Church, a beautiful building in Perpendicular style. The inscription beside the tomb is a copy of that on the Queen's coffin.

The grounds of the castle are superb, including the remains of a medieval tithe barn and a lake, home to imported wildfowl. The formal gardens include the Queen's Garden, named for Katherine Parr though not in existence during her time here, and the Knot Garden, which takes its name and design from a dress of Queen Elizabeth I depicted in one of the castle's paintings. Regularly during the summer Sudeley is the site of exhibitions and craft displays, details of which may be found in local tourist offices.

On the opposite side of Winchcombe from Sudeley Castle is **Prescott**, famous throughout the motoring world as the location of hill trials up the steep side of Nottingham Hill. The village is home to the Bugatti Trust, set up in 1987 to honour Ettore Bugatti (1881–1947) one of the greatest names in motoring. The Trust has an exhibition, with models, photographs and complete cars, telling the story of Bugatti and his cars, and a library with a photographic and document archive that is available for research.

The Cotswold Way enters Winchcombe along the Pilgrims' Way, a route once trodden by medieval pilgrims making their way between the sacred remains of St. Kenelm and the Holy Blood of Hailes Abbey. Today's visitor can use the B4632 (passing a turning to Winchcombe Pottery, where hand-made pottery, some fired in an old bottle kiln, is sold on a site which also includes other craftworkers).

Hailes Abbey was founded in 1245 by Richard, Earl of Cornwall, three years after he had vowed to do so if his life were spared during a storm at sea. Richard was returning from a crusade in the Holy Land and it looked as though his ship would be wrecked off the Scillies. The ship made port safely and on land granted to him by his brother Henry II Richard endowed an abbey for Cistercian monks. The Abbey was dedicated in 1251 in the presence of King Henry and Queen Eleanor, his wife.

Hailes' early history was uneventful, but all that changed in 1270 when Richard's son Edmund presented the Abbey with phial of Holy Blood. Edmund had himself endowed an abbey at Ashbridge and he gave a second phial to the abbot there. The Holy Blood, which came with a certificate of authentication from the Patriarch of Jerusalem (later Pope Urban IV), had been bought by Edmund at the Flanders court.

The existence of the Holy Blood brought an immediate and sharp improvement in Hailes' prosperity. It was placed in a large

shrine at the eastern end of the Abbey church, set at the focus
of a half-circle of five chapels, the whole probably designed to
represent the Crown of Thorns, and to allow pilgrims to process
around the shrine. Soon Hailes became one of the most important pilgrimage sites in Britain, so well-known that Chaucer
even included the solemn oath 'I swere by the blode of Christ
that is in Hayles' in one of his *Canterbury Tales*. But though the
relic brought the Abbey great fame and wealth, it did not protect the monks from all the rigours of medieval Britain: in 1271
the Abbey was almost destroyed by fire and in 1361 the community was virtually wiped out by the Black Death.

Hailes was dissolved on Christmas Eve, 1539, the day after
the dissolution of Winchcombe Abbey. But the Holy Blood
had been confiscated a few weeks before. It was taken to London for examination and exposed as not only a fake but also as
having been used in an elaborate fraud to extort money from
pilgrims – although it has to be remembered that the exposers
were enemies of the monasteries. It was said that the blood was
actually honey coloured with saffron and that it had been kept
in a glass container that was transparent on one side, opaque
on the other. A monk would show the container to a pilgrim,
presenting its opaque side and telling him that persons in mor-
tal sin could not see the blood. When the pilgrim had paid for

Hailes Abbey.

absolution, sleight of hand was used to turn the container, allowing the, now absolved, pilgrim to 'miraculously' see it.

Following the dissolution, Hailes was stripped of everything valuable, including the roof lead. Open to the elements the Abbey soon decayed. A new owner demolished the church, but renovated one section as a house. Sadly, in the early eighteenth century this part too was destroyed. Today all that remain are the foundations and some arcades of the cloisters – enough to give an idea of the whole and an evocative reminder of its great days. There is also a museum exploring the history of the Abbey and housing some of the better pieces of stone recovered from the site. The ruins are now in the hands of English Heritage.

Opposite the abbey ruins is **Hailes Church**, an undistinguished looking building housing the finest medieval wall paintings still to be found in the Cotswolds. The church is twelfth-century, pre-dating the Abbey, the murals probably dating from the four-teenth century. They are likely to have been saved from destruction by the Puritans by having been covered with a layer of plaster some time before the Civil War; the careful removal of the plaster allowed them to be restored. The compositions are a quite surprising departure from the more usual religious themes, but are masterpieces of Renaissance-like naturalness.

Hailes Church.

A GWR Train at Toddington Station.

Further along the B4632, to the right, lies the Gloucestershire and Warwickshire Railway. The railway, entirely run by volunteer enthusiasts, uses a section of the line that once linked Cheltenham to Stratford-upon-Avon by way of Winchcombe and Broadway. At present the line is open through the 634m (688yd) Greet Tunnel, to the north-west of Winchcombe, to Gotherington, a distance of 8km (5 miles) (though 16km journeys are actually made as boarding/unloading is not allowed at Gotherington at present). The trains use steam engines and run on a scheduled timetable throughout the year (but more often in summer). It is hoped that eventually the line will be completely reopened. The site (the initial letters of which are GWR, a happy coincidence, this having been a Great Western Railway line) also offers visitors the chance to drive a train, and has a shop with enough souvenirs and books to keep any train lover occupied for hours. There is also a steam-hauled narrow gauge (2ft) railway operated by the enthusiasts of the North Gloucestershire Railway Group.

A Short tour of Bredon Hill

From the roundabout just beyond the railway site our tour of spring-line villages turns right for Stanway, but before going that way a left turn allows a circuit of **Bredon Hill** to be made. A casual glance at a map of the area might lead you to assume that the individual who defined the Cotswold AONB had lost his way. But that is not the case. The Cotswolds were created by the uplifting of a limestone block, the block's scarp face then eroding. Bredon Hill is a part of that block, being an 'outlier', a detached block caused by differential erosion of the limestone. In our journey southwards we shall see other outliers and outliers-in-the-making.

The first village reached is **Toddington**, where a right turn leads to the church of St. Leonard, built in about 1870 by G.E. Street, one of the better Victorian church architects. The church replaced an earlier one dedicated to St.Thomas à Becket built, it is thought, by the Tracey family, lords of the manor, to expunge the guilt of one of their members William de Tracey, one of the four knights who murdered Becket. The church, with its excellent spire, houses the superb tomb, in white marble, of Charles Hanbury-Tracey and his wife, the pair reclining in effigy. Beside the church are the ruins of an early manor house of the Traceys. The present house, also dating from Victorian times, stands to the north in parkland that extends to almost 200ha (500 acres).

Continuing along the B4077, turn right for **Alderton**, which has half-timbered as well as Cotswold stone houses. The pleasant little church, built in the fourteenth century, was gutted by Victorian restorers. Now head for Beckford, passing a turning, to the left, to **Little Washbourne**, which has a delightful little Norman church with a double-decker pulpit and eighteenth-century box pews. **Great Washbourne** was once 'owned' by Sir Adrian Fortescue who attended Henry VIII's wedding to Anne Boleyn, but denied that the King could be head of the church and lost his own head as a result.

Beckford was once home to an Augustinian Priory whose church is still the parish church. Here, at Beckford Silk, visitors can watch the hand-printing of silk as well as buy exclusive designs in scarves and ties. Although Beckford's silk is imported from China, the industry is a link with former times in the Cotswolds, there having been a thriving silk milling industry in the north of the area in the eighteenth and nineteenth centuries. A little further on, at **Conderton**, there is a studio where visitors may watch, by contrast, the hand-painting of silk in a converted barn and buy a range of articles from ties and scarves to cushions and pictures. The studio has a shop in Broadway. The village also has a craft pottery, operated by Toff Milway, where the process of hand-making may be seen and the salt-glazed finished product bought.

Nearby **Overbury**, with its half-timbered houses, is claimed to be one of the prettiest villages in Worcestershire. It lies below Bredon Hill which can be climbed by a path which goes through the parkland surrounding Overbury Court. On the summit of the hill (at 295m, 960ft) is Parson's Folly, an eighteenth-century tower built by a Kemerton man called Parson in the centre of an Iron Age hillfort. Excavation of the fort revealed the mutilated bodies of about fifty men who, it is speculated, died in battle around 2,000 years ago. The bodies had not been buried, but left exposed, to be covered (eventually) by windblown earth. Close to the Tower and also within the hillfort's ditches is the Banbury Stone, a huge slab of rock.

Silk painting, Conderton.

Toff Milway's Pottery Shop, Conderton.

Although legend has it that the stone was associated with druidic sacrifices and that it descends to drink from the River Avon if it hears the bells of Pershore Abbey strike twelve, it is no more than a natural boulder, as are the nearby ones and the so-called King and Queen Stones (three in number despite the name) which stand below the summit. Close to Overbury is **Kemerton** where at The Priory there is a superb garden with herbaceous borders planted in colour groups and a sunken garden.

Beyond Kemerton the tour around Bredon Hill goes through Bredon, which lies outside the AONB, but is notable for its fourteenth-century tithe barn, 44m (144ft) long with superb porches. The barn is in the care of the National Trust. Now head north towards Evesham, turning right to reach **Great Comberton**, with another good collection of half-timbered houses and a dovecote with the largest number of nest holes (1,524) in Britain. Continue through Little Comberton to reach **Elmley Castle**, named for a Norman castle destroyed by Henry VII. According to legend, Queen Elizabeth I once stayed in the village (though clearly not at the castle) on her way from Worcester to London.

Round the eastern end of Bredon Hill to reach Ashton-under-Hill. Ahead now are Dumbleton and the Alderton Hills, lower outliers of the Cotswold plateau. Go through the village of Dumbleton and continue to **Wormington** where the church contains a rare Saxon crucifix.

Ashton-under-Hill.

Close to Hailes Abbey is **Didbrook**, the first of the 'spring line' villages, settlements that grew up near the base of the scarp slope where rain falling on the high wolds re-emerged as springs. The village is notable for several cruck-frame buildings, an early constructional method which used huge timbers in an inverted 'V' to form the basic structure of the house. The church is also interesting. It is not original, that one having been pulled down by the outraged villagers after prisoners from the Battle of Tewkesbury (fought in 1471 during the Wars of the Roses) had been herded into it and murdered. The door, taken from the original church, is still marked by bullet holes. The church is also unusual in having its tower rise from ground level, with three arches in the nave.

Close to Didbrook is **Stanway**, reached beyond an unusual war memorial with a bronze statue of St. George and the Dragon. Stanway House, one of the finest in the Cotswolds, lies beyond an impressive gatehouse, once thought to be the work of Inigo Jones but now believed to be by Timothy Strong, a Cotswold mason from a family whose work included St. Paul's Cathedral. The House is Jacobean with superb windows and gables, built in a golden stone that seems to glow in the evening light. Surrounding the house are outbuildings constructed with the same elegance, the best being a huge fourteenth-century tithe barn.

The House was one of the last to have been built with a Great Hall, where the owners and their servants ate together. In later houses the servants were generally confined 'below stairs'. The House is filled with furniture which is worth a visit on its own: look out for the Chinese day beds in Chippendale style. The grounds, too, are excellent. In addition to the outbuildings there is an eighteenth-century stone pyramid from which a waterfall once poured, and a brewery which produces a beer (called Stanny after the local pronunciation of the village name) much in demand in nearby inns. Behind the pyramid there is a dog's cemetery full of curious epitaphs. The House was built by the Tracey family who have owned the site for

The Entrance to Stanway House, with the village church behind.

about a thousand years. One member of the family, Sir William, who died in 1530, was a Protestant when the country was Catholic and left a will which was deemed Protestant and heretical by the Archbishop of Canterbury who was so incensed that he demanded that the writer be burned at the stake. The fact that Tracey was already dead and buried did nothing to placate the outraged prelate who insisted on Sir William's body being dug up and burned.

Other residents of the house had influences on British literature, one, Dr Robert Dover, was the rescuer of Alexander Selkirk, the model for Defoe's Robinson Crusoe, and another was J.M. Barrie. It is said that Barrie awoke one night and saw a moonbeam playing on the wall of his bedroom, this being the inspiration for Tinkerbell in Peter Pan. It is to Barrie, a life-long cricket fan, that Stanway owns the superb thatched pavilion that stands across the road from the House. It rests on staddle stones, a characteristic form of Cotswold damp-and-rodent-proofing.

The road between the House and the cricket pitch passes through pleasant country to reach **Stanton**, another showpiece village of honey-coloured stone houses. Stanton owes its remarkable state of preservation – it is of almost entirely seventeenth-century construction – to the efforts of Sir Philip Stott who bought most of the village properties in 1906 and resisted, until his death in 1937, all attempts at modernization. Later owners have maintained the village free of the twentieth-century amenities so common elsewhere. Stott lived at Stanton Court, built during James I's reign, but considerably altered in the seventeenth century. The village cross, too, is seventeenth century, but the nearby church is older, some parts remaining from the original twelfth-century building. Inside, look for the deep gouges in the pew ends: these were made by chains at a time when dogs accompanied their owners to services.

From Stanton head back to the B4632, turning right towards Broadway. Soon turnings are reached on the right to Laverton and **Buckland**, exquisite tiny villages. The east window of Buckland Church is said by many to be the best in the Cotswolds. William Morris was so impressed he paid for it to be re-leaded while he was staying at nearby Broadway Tower. The church also has six carved stones with painted panels which are thought to have come from Hailes Abbey. The nearby Rectory, sadly no longer open to the public, is fifteenth century, probably the oldest in the country and until recently still in use.

Broadway, beyond Buckland, is one of the Cotswolds' major tourist centres. The village's name is immediately obvious to the visitor, Broadway consisting of one long, broad street heading towards the scarp edge from the village green. In summer this long street is often choked with traffic, but a bypass (under construction at the time of writing) will soon ease the problem. The street's width is, in part, due to the covering of two streams that run down either side of the High Street. Until early this century dip holes remained in the

Broadway.

stream covers, allowing the villagers to collect water with buckets. The focal point for most villages is the church, but in Broadway's case that is not true, the church lying some way out of the village along the road to Snowshill. It is dedicated to St. Eadburgha, a Saxon princess and grand-daughter of Alfred the Great, and was built in the twelfth century. The church close to the village green was built about 1840 so that the villagers had less far to walk.

Close to the Green, on its far side from the High Street, is The Grange, built in the early fourteenth century for the Abbot of Pershore. The Prior of Worcester also had a house here – Prior's Manse at the far end of the High Street (close to the turn for the car park) – which dates from the same time despite the 'modern' look of its gables and dormers. The two houses are among the oldest in Worcestershire. Between these two Broadway has an array of beautiful houses, many now taken over by craft and souvenir outlets. Of the crafts shops the most famous is that of Gordon Russell, the furniture maker. One of the most notable buildings is the Lygon Arms.

During the eighteenth and the nineteenth centuries Broadway prospered as a staging post on the coach road between Worcester and London, horses being changed here before the climb up Fish Hill. Of the houses that date from this period the Lygon Arms is the most impressive. It was originally the White Horse Inn, but changed its name when the former butler of General Lygon bought it. Lygon had fought at Waterloo, the butler's choice of his name being a shrewd piece of commercialism, especially since Lygon had trees planted on his estate, at nearby Springhill, according to the troop deployment at Waterloo and would often stride between them refighting the battle. At the height of its coaching success Broadway had around twenty inns in addition to the Lygon Arms.

Close to the Lygon Arms is the Teddy Bear Museum, which explores the history of the bears, with many old and curious examples. The collection, which also includes dolls and toys, is claimed to be the largest in Britain.

Today's car-borne visitor will find Fish Hill an easier climb than did the horses hauling the coaches towards London. Near the Fish Inn at the top of the hill (named, it is believed, for the sign of three fishes, an early Christian symbol, that was inscribed on a priest's house that once stood here) there was once a sign telling coachmen where to unharness the extra horses that had been taken on for the climb. Opposite the inn is a car park and picnic site from where there are expansive views over the Vale of Evesham. On the other side of the inn is Broadway Tower, now the focus of a country park.

The 20m (65ft) tower was built in 1799 for the Earl of Coventry at the request of his wife. She is said to have been impressed that she could see a bonfire lit on the spot and wanted the tower as a permanent reminder. The Tower's position (at 310m, 1,024ft, the second highest point in the Cotswolds) is certainly an impressive look-out: before the redrawing of county boundaries thirteen counties could be seen from the top. Today it is a mere twelve. The architect James Wyatt decided to use a dark, rather than a local stone so that the tower would look 'Saxon', repairs in local stone

Broadway Tower.

being very obvious as a result. The Tower is famous for having been the temporary home of, most significantly, William Morris, but also many Pre-Raphaelite artists such as Dante Gabriel Rossetti and Edward Burne-Jones. Morris wrote the letter forming the Society for the Protection of Ancient Buildings at the Tower. He was a life-long lover of the Cotswolds, living the latter part of his life at Kelmscott Manor, near Lechlade, just outside the AONB. His interest in crafts as well as the arts was instrumental in the development of the craft industries which are now such a feature of the area. The Tower has an exhibition on Morris, as well as on its own history.

In the Country Park around the Tower there are red deer and the now rare Cotswold sheep, an adventure playground, picnic and barbecue sites and a restaurant.

From the Fish Inn, continue along the A44 to reach a crossroads, with the B4081 to Chipping Campden on your left. The signpost here, erected in 1669, is one of the oldest in the country and marks the spot where one of the gravest injustices in British history took place, the execution of three people for a murder that did not occur.

William Harrison, a steward to Lady Noel of Chipping Campden, disappeared on 16 August 1660 while collecting her rents. As he had been a faithful servant for over fifty years, and was nearly seventy years old, foul play was suspected. Harrison's wife sent John Perry, their manservant, to look for her husband, but Perry too disappeared. The next day Harrison's son Edward began to search and found Perry, who could offer no explanation of where he had been all night. Edward Harrison and Perry continued the search, soon finding William's blood-stained comb and hatband. No other trace of William was found. Under questioning John Perry now began to tell increasingly confused and weird stories, eventually confessing that he had murdered Harrison with the help of his mother Joan and brother Richard. They had, John Perry said, thrown the body in the millpond. The pond was searched, but no body was found. Despite this Joan and Richard Perry, vigorously protesting their innocence, were arrested. The first judge to hear the case threw out the charge of murder on the grounds that there was no body, but at a second trial in 1661 with a less scrupulous judge, the three were found guilty and sentenced to hang. At their execution on this spot, the pleas of Joan and Richard to John to acknowledge their innocence were so heartfelt that even the crowd joined in. John remained passive as the two were hanged. Only then did he protest his own innocence, but to no avail. The three bodies were left to rot in chains as an example to others, and what was left of them was still there the next year when William Harrison walked back into his house. His story of being kidnapped and taken to Turkey where he was sold as a slave, of escape and a cross-European journey on foot with dangers at every step was clearly nonsense even for a man who was not over seventy and in poor health. The truth will never be known, but it is likely that Harrison was stealing from Lady Noel and planned his disappearance to cover the thefts. If that was true then Harrison must have known of the trial and executions. But he never changed his story, remaining in Lady Noel's employment until his death some ten years later. The only pointer to his guilt is the fact that his wife hanged herself shortly after his return; perhaps she had been told the truth.

Turn left at the signpost to reach **Chipping Campden**.

ADDRESSES AND OPENING TIMES

Winchcombe

FOLK AND POLICE MUSEUM,
Town Hall *(01242 602925)*

❖

OPEN: April–Oct, Mon–Sat, 10.00am–5.00pm

RAILWAY MUSEUM,
23 Gloucester Street *(01242 620641)*

❖

OPEN: Good Friday–Oct, Sat, Sun and Bank Holidays,
10.00am–5.00pm; daily during school holidays

SUDELEY CASTLE AND GARDENS,
near Winchcombe *(01242 604357)*

❖

OPEN: 1 March–Easter, Gardens only, daily,
10.00am–4.30pm; Easter–Oct, Gardens, daily,
10.00am–5.30pm; Castle daily, 11.00am–5.00pm

THE BUGATTI TRUST,
Prescott Hall, Gotherington *(01242 677201)*

❖

OPEN: all year, Mon–Fri, 10.00am–3.30pm

HAILES ABBEY,
near Winchcombe *(01242 602398)*

❖

OPEN: Easter–Oct, daily 10.00am–6.00pm (dusk in Oct);
Nov–Easter, Wed–Sun, 10.00am–1.30pm, 2.00–4.00pm;
closed on Bank Holiday

GLOUCESTERSHIRE–WARWICKSHIRE RAILWAY,
Toddington, near Winchcombe *(01242 621405)*

❖

OPEN: site facilities open Sat, Sun, 11.00am–5.00pm and on
days trains run; trains run all year; timetable adjusted annually

NORTH GLOUCESTERSHIRE RAILWAY,
Toddington, near Winchcombe
❖
OPEN: Easter–Sept, Sun and Bank Holidays,
12.00am–5.00pm

Bredon Hill

BECKFORD SILK,
Beckford *(01386 8811507)*
❖
OPEN: all year except 24 Dec–2 Jan, Mon–Sat,
9.00am–5.30pm

ELAINE RIPPON HAND-PAINTED SILK STUDIO,
Darkes House, Conderton *(01386 725289)*
❖
OPEN: Feb–Dec, Mon–Sat, 10.00am–5.00pm;
Jan, Sat, 10.00am–5.00pm;
closed 24 Dec–1st Sat in Jan

TOFF MILWAY'S CONDERTON POTTERY,
The Old Forge, Conderton *(01386 725387)*
❖
OPEN: all year, Mon–Sat, 9.00am–5.00pm

THE PRIORY,
Kemerton *(01386 725258)*
❖
OPEN: June–Sept, Fri, 2.00–7.00pm; also occasional
Sundays, ring for details

TITHE BARN (National Trust),
Bredon *(01684 850051)*
❖
OPEN: Apr–Nov, Wed, Thurs, Sat and Sun,
10.00am–6.00pm (or dusk); Dec–Feb by appointment only

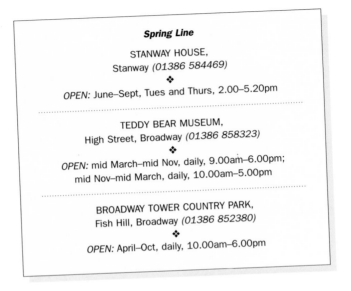

Spring Line

STANWAY HOUSE,
Stanway *(01386 584469)*

❖

OPEN: June–Sept, Tues and Thurs, 2.00–5.20pm

. . . .

TEDDY BEAR MUSEUM,
High Street, Broadway *(01386 858323)*

❖

OPEN: mid March–mid Nov, daily, 9.00am–6.00pm;
mid Nov–mid March, daily, 10.00am–5.00pm

. . . .

BROADWAY TOWER COUNTRY PARK,
Fish Hill, Broadway *(01386 852380)*

❖

OPEN: April–Oct, daily, 10.00am–6.00pm

Chipping Campden

Many would agree, with justification, that Chipping Campden is the finest of all Cotswold towns. As a market (Chipping derives from *ceping*, the old word for a market) the town grew rich on wool, being a leading centre for its sale, the rich wool merchants of the day building houses here and endowing a church that is certainly one of the three finest 'wool churches'. (The others, by common consent, are at Northleach and Cirencester.) When the wool industry declined, Chipping Campden failed to find an alternative activity and the loss of its prosperity meant that it became a time capsule of medieval architecture. That, together with the refusal of the town to give itself wholeheartedly to tourism in the way that nearby Broadway has (no criticism either way is intended here, just a statement of the position), means that the visitor is rewarded with a stroll through a townscape virtually unchanged for several hundred years.

St. James's Church was built in Perpendicular style in the fourteenth century, with a tall tower (36m, 120ft) topped by

The Market Hall, Chipping Campden.

(Right) St. James's Church, Chipping Campden.

twelve pinnacles, for the Apostles, a number mirrored in the avenue of twelve lime trees along the walkway. So perfect is the outside of the church that it can be difficult to tear yourself away, but even greater riches lie within. The cope of crimson velvet is one of the few that survive from the reign of Richard II, while the late fifteenth-century altar cloths in embroidered white silk damask

53

are the only perfect set in existence; but it is the memorials that most people come to see. That to William Grevel and his wife is the largest memorial brass in the area. Grevel, who died in 1401, was the richest merchant of his day; it was he who presented the church with the cope. Grevel is depicted in the short hair and forked beard that was the 'uniform' of a fourteenth-century merchant. His fame spread far from the Cotswolds and it has even been suggested that he was the model for Chaucer's merchant in the *Canterbury Tales*. Another fine memorial, in stone, is to Thomas Smith, lord of the manor and a gentleman of Henry VIII's court. Smith lies in full knight's insignia surrounded by the kneeling figures of his two wives and thirteen children. If Smith's memorial seems excessive, move on to the South Chapel, built to house the remains of the family and successors of Sir Baptist Hicks. Hicks was a London merchant who moved to the Cotswolds to increase his wealth and become fabulously rich, so rich that he was able to finance King James I. He also built the houses in London in what is now Campden Hill Square. In Chipping Campden his house beside the church was of such ostentatious splendour that the locals, who were used to seeing inordinate displays of wealth by rich merchants, actually took exception to it. As a comparison, Hicks built the town's Market Hall for £90 but spent £29,000 on his own house and a further £15,000 on furnishings. When the house was garrisoned by Royalist forces in 1645 (about thirty years after its completion), there was a mysterious fire and it was completely destroyed.

But by then Sir Baptist had been dead for several years and lay beneath the tomb in the South Chapel, on top of which his alabaster effigy lies, with that of his wife in their state robes. The tomb, though elaborate, is restrained in comparison with that of their daughter Juliana and her husband Sir Edward Noel (the employers of William Harrison) who are portrayed upright, larger-than-life-size and in shrouds as they step from their tombs on Judgement Day. More delicate is the memorial to Penelope Hicks, a daughter of Sir Edward and Juliana, who died of blood poisoning when just twenty-two years old after pricking her finger on an embroidery needle.

From the church, go along Church Street. The ornate gateway to the left is virtually all that now remains of Sir Baptist Hicks's house. Further on, to the right, set on a raised pavement, are the almshouses, presented to the town by Sir Baptist in 1612. They were built for six poor men and six poor women, and, with

Lady Elizabeth Hicks, St. James's Church, Chipping Campden.

their tall chimneys, are a delight. Opposite them is a walled dip where carts would soak their wheels to prevent their drying, shrinking and losing their hoops. Bear right by the fourteenth-century Eight Bells Inn to reach the High Street. To the right from here is the old village pump and the Ernest Wilson Memorial Garden, named in honour of the Campden-born plant collector, famous for the introduction of many species of oriental (particularly Chinese) shrubs and trees to the west. Wilson, born in 1876, became the director of Harvard University's Arnold Arboretum and died in the USA.

Turn left along the High Street. Immediately on the right is Grevel's House built in 1380 for William Grevel. The house has remained virtually unchanged for over 600 years and still houses his office. The double-bay windows are an extremely rare feature of Cotswold houses of that period.

To the left is Woolstaplers' Hall. This was built at much the same time as Grevel's House for Robert Calf, another wool merchant, but takes its name from its later use as the meeting place for merchants of raw fleeces, then known as staples. Merchants from as far away as Florence came to the Hall to buy. Close to the Hall is Bedfont House, the best of the town's eighteenth-century houses.

Continue along the High Street to reach the Market Hall and the Town Hall which stand in the centre of the street. As noted earlier, the Market Hall was given to the town by Sir Baptist Hicks – 'for the sale of butter, cheese and poultry'. It is a beautiful building, its complex roofs held aloft by Cotswold stone pillars. The Town Hall is a more curious building. It has fourteenth-century origins and retains panelled buttresses from that time, legend having it that they are the remnants of a chapel to St. Catherine built by Hugh de Gondeville, a local knight who led the gang of four which murdered Thomas à Becket. The story is that de Gondeville built the chapel to expunge his guilt, but no incontrovertible evidence for this has been discovered.

Turn left along Sheep Street to reach, to the right, the Old Silk Mill, the home of the town's famous Guild of Handicrafts. The Guild was founded by C.R. Ashbee who moved to Chipping Campden in 1902. The Guild failed

Neil Jordan working at his Silk Mill studio, Chipping Campden.

in 1907, but George Hart stayed on in the Mill. Today the rejuvenated Guild is still there and D.T. Hart, a company of silversmiths run by descendants of George Hart, still operates there, as do a small number of other craftworkers, including the Pyments cabinetmakers – Jim Pyment, a Canadian having helped to re-establish the Guild. Robert Welch, the silversmith and designer, another co-founder of the new Guild, has a shop on the corner of Sheep Street and High Street.

ADDRESSES AND OPENING TIMES

D.T. HART (silversmith); DIANE HASSALL (shoes);
NEIL JORDAN (silver jewellery),
The Silk Mill, Sheep Street,
Chipping Campden *(01386 841100)*
❖
OPEN: all year, Mon–Fri, 9.00am–5.30pm;
Sat, 9.00–12.00am

ROBERT WELCH (silverware and cutlery),
Lower High Street, Chipping Campden
❖
OPEN: all year, Mon–Sat, 9.30am–5.30pm;
Sun, 11.00am–4.00pm

ANN SMITH (jewellery and enamel),
Peacock House, Chipping Campden
(01386 840879)
❖
OPEN: all year, Mon–Sat, 9.30am–5.00pm
(telephone first)

MARTIN GOTREL (jewellery),
The Square, Chipping Campden
(01386 841360)
❖
OPEN: all year, Tues–Sat, 10.00am–5.30pm

A Short Tour from Chipping Campden

From the western end of the town, take the steep road towards Dover's Hill, soon reaching a crossroads. To the left from here, buried in the vegetation on the right-hand side of the road, is the Kiftsgate Stone, a somewhat nondescript stone, but one which, together with others of its kind, has given the English language one of its most enduring clichés, for the stone is a moot point. At such places the locals would gather to discuss matters of common concern or hear important announcements. The site would always be near a prominent track – here the stone is on the *Chief's Geat*, 'geat' being Saxon for a track. The proclamation of George III is the last public announcement known to have been made from the stone.

Go straight across at the crossroads to reach, to the right, Dover's Hill. The hill is named for Robert Dover of Campden (though Norfolk-born) who, through the assistance of his friend Endymion Porter, a courtier of James I, gained royal agreement to regenerate games which had been held at Whitsun from Saxon times, on an *ad hoc* basis, on the hill. The games were advertised as *Dr Robert Dover's Olympick Games* and began with a great flourish: a gun was fired from a makeshift castle and Dover himself rode out on a white horse, wearing a velvet suit with a white feather in his hat. The games included such Cotswold favourites as singlestick fight (when the two opponents attempted to smash each other's skulls with a long stick held in one

Dover's Hill.

58

hand, the other hand tucked into their waist belts) and shin-kicking, in which the opponents did as the name implies, until one cried enough. There are stories of competitors hardening their shins by beating them with planks or hammers; it was even suggested that deal made the best shin-hardening plank, though why it was deemed so is not recorded. There were also more refined events – horse and foot races and chess – and a hare-coursing competition. The games were famous in their day, even Shakespeare had heard of them, having Slender ask Page, 'How does your fallow greyhound, Sir? I heard he was out-run on Cotsall' in *The Merry Wives of Windsor*.

The Civil War ended the games, the Puritans disapproving of such frivolity but they were revived after the Restoration. They were stopped in 1853 after they had become an excuse for drunken brawling, but were revived again in 1951 as part of the Festival of Britain celebrations, though the more masochistic of the sports have been dropped. Visitors at times other than the weekend towards the end of May when the games are held (on a Friday and Saturday, the latter being the day of Chipping Campden's annual Scuttlebrook Wake), will find the hill quiet apart from a few walkers (some perhaps starting or finishing the Cotswold Way which links Bath and Chipping Campden). The view from the hill, where the Cotswold Edge turns sharply eastward, is superb.

Continuing past the turn to Dover's Hill you will descend into **Weston Subedge** where the houses reflect the fact that the Cotswolds are coming to an end. Bishop William Latimer, a friend of Sir Thomas More, once lived in the village perhaps in the house now named for him. To the left from Weston are **Saintbury and Willersley**, the former with a beautifully positioned church and some excellent seventeenth-century houses, the latter with a lovely little duckpond.

To the right the main road passes **Aston Subedge**, home of Robert Dover's friend Endymion Porter, to reach **Mickleton** and two magnificent gardens. **Kiftsgate Court Garden** surrounds a largely Victorian house which was bought in 1918 by the Muirs, Heather Muir, setting out to create a garden from what had become a virtual wilderness. Mrs Muir was assisted by her daughter Diany Binny and she, in turn, by her daughter Anne Chambers, so that the garden we see today is the work of three generations of gardeners. The garden, in part formal with a fountain and steps and in part more traditionally English, is beautiful, particularly the terraced areas and the rose gardens. The latter include the species Rose Filipes Kiftsgate, claimed to be the largest rose grown in Britain.

Kiftsgate Court Garden.

Hidcote Manor Garden lies a short distance to the east of Kiftsgate Court, near the hamlet of Hidcote Bartrim. When Major Lawrence Johnston (who was born in Paris in 1871 of American parents, but took British citizenship so as to be able to fight in the Boer War) bought the Manor is 1905 there was a house, with eleven acres of neglect. Over the next forty-three years Johnston, one of the country's leading horticulturists, transformed the garden into one of the best in Britain. It is not one garden but many,

Hidcote Manor Gardens.

60

Johnston using formal hedges to separate areas which he developed individually, forming the Fuchsia Garden, the White Garden, the Pool Garden and so on. Clever designs create a range of colours at different times of the year and ever-changing colour shapes within the gardens. In 1948 Johnston gave Hidcote Manor to the National Trust who now maintain it true to the design principles he laid down.

To the north of Mickleton lies Meon Hill, positively the last remnant of Cotswold and, hardly surprisingly given its position, topped by an Iron Age hillfort. Nearby **Ilmington**, a somewhat struggling village, but with some very attractive houses, is the last village within the AONB. Its church, Norman and with a fine sixteenth-century porch, has oak carvings by Robert Thompson, the early twentieth-century master carver from Kilburn in Yorkshire. Thompson's trademark was the mouse which he carved on to all of his pieces: it is traditional for visitors to discover the eleven mice that find a home in the church.

From Ilmington head south-west to return to Chipping Campden, passing a turn to **Ebrington** (known as Yubberton to the locals) whose cottages – of stone, but usually thatched – are yet more evidence that Cotswold country has reached its northern limit.

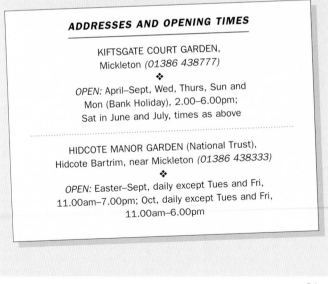

ADDRESSES AND OPENING TIMES

KIFTSGATE COURT GARDEN,
Mickleton *(01386 438777)*
❖
OPEN: April–Sept, Wed, Thurs, Sun and
Mon (Bank Holiday), 2.00–6.00pm;
Sat in June and July, times as above

HIDCOTE MANOR GARDEN (National Trust),
Hidcote Bartrim, near Mickleton *(01386 438333)*
❖
OPEN: Easter–Sept, daily except Tues and Fri,
11.00am–7.00pm; Oct, daily except Tues and Fri,
11.00am–6.00pm

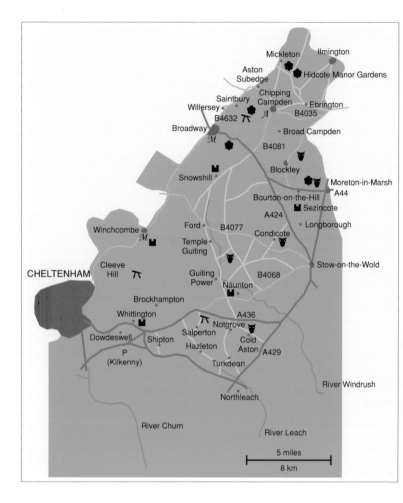

TOUR 2: Chipping Campden to Cheltenham: Wold Villages

The journey from Cheltenham to Chipping Campden passes so much of interest that the suggested return, across the high wolds might be better considered as a separate tour.

From Chipping Campden, head south to **Broad Campden**, a pretty village whose Victorian church is, according to Pevsner, 'better outside than in'. A derelict Norman chapel here was restored by C.R. Ashbee who lived there until 1917. The village's Quaker Meeting House was established in 1663, shortly after George Fox had founded the Society of Friends. Beyond the village the road climbs, then passes Northwick Park, fine parkland around a late seventeenth-century mansion, now converted into flats, before reaching **Blockley**, another of north Cotswolds' collection of beautiful villages.

Blockley's position, tucked into a tight hollow through which rushes the Knee Brook, made it ideal for the washing of the fleeces from sheep grazing the local high wolds. The villagers

Broad Campden.

63

must have counted their blessings when the high clerics of Worcester demolished other villages, to the north-east and the south-west, to make way for more sheep, scattering their inhabitants. But Blockley's prosperity was not to last, the decline in the wool industry bringing great hardship. But the fast-running Knee Brook was again the village's salvation: by the mid-nineteenth century its waters were powering six silk mills in the village, some of them producing raw ribbon for the Coventry ribbon factories. By the 1880s this industry, too, had declined, now its only echoes are the names of the mills – Old Silk Mill and Ribbon Mill – which have been converted into private residences.

At its height the silk industry employed several hundred people, a prosperity reflected in the church which, though originally twelfth-century Norman, was expanded and restored each time Blockley's fortunes improved. The tower was completed only in 1725. Inside there is a fine pulpit and two very good brasses commemorating priests. The earlier of these is

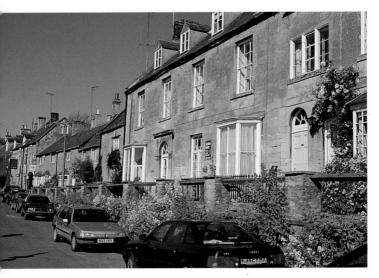

Blockley.

dated 1485: that of William Neele, who died in 1510, is unique in showing the kneeling priest in the full vestments for the Mass. There is also a collection of memorials to the Rushout family who lived at nearby Northwick Park. John Rushout, the second Lord Northwick, was a friend of both Lord Nelson and Sir William Hamilton, the husband of the Admiral's mistress. It was he who laid out the Five Mile Drive, an avenue now taken, in part, by the A44 to the west of Blockley.

A walk through the village is worthwhile, the well-kept cottages alive with colour when the gardens and hanging baskets are in bloom. Look for the difference between the terraced cottages of the silk weavers and the detached houses of the mill owners (a difference that has become less clear-cut as any house in Blockley is now a very desirable residence). Look, too, for Fish Cottage (on the main road, close to the church) named for the grave of a fish. As the epitaph records, the fish, a trout, lived in the pond in the cottage's garden for twenty years and was eventually so tame it would feed from the cottage owner's hand. It was killed in 1865, probably by a jealous neighbour who clubbed it to death.

Not far from Blockley is the Great Western Inn, a slightly optimistic name as when the railway was built from Worcester to Oxford it passed a couple of miles north-east of the town. From the inn head towards Paxford, and then turn right towards Draycott to reach the **Sleepy Hollow Farm Park** where visitors may see both farm and wild animals ranging from big cats to Arctic foxes. There is a pet centre, a children's play area and opportunities for shire-drawn cart rides. The Farm Park has a regular annual calendar of events ranging from lambing to exhibitions of exotic pets. Details are available from local tourist offices or at the Park.

To the east of Blockley lies the pleasant village of **Aston Magna**, with the remains of a moat to the south of the church. This is believed to have once protected a grange of the Bishops of Worcester. When one considers their clearances of local villages the Bishops probably needed the protection.

Head to the south from Blockley, taking the B4479 to reach the A44. Turn left to reach **Bourton-on-the-Hill**, aptly named as the village tumbles down the hill beside the main road (which follows the line of an old turnpike). The noise and traffic aside, Bourton is a beautiful village, its cottages the equal of anything in quieter Blockley. At the eastern end of the village, at the bottom of the hill, is a fine, and huge, tithe barn with

Bourton-on-the-Hill.

seven arches. The barn, inscribed with the date of its construction 1570, retains its original massive roof timbers.

The village church is a pleasant building, worth visiting to see its rare Winchester measures. Before 1587 the system of weights and measures in Britain was haphazard, but in that year Elizabeth I granted a charter to Winchester making the city's official weights and measures the standard throughout the country. As a consequence, magistrates' clerks had to obtain standard weights and measures for use in disputes over corn, fleeces and other commodities. St. Lawrence's Church preserves two such standard measures, a bushel (8 gallons) and a peck (2 gallons) made in bell metal. The measures are inscribed with the name of the clerk to the Bourton bench Frederick Francis Findon and the date, 1816. The date is significant for the rarity value: within ten years Imperial standards had replaced Winchester standards and the two pieces had become obsolete.

The Cotswold Falconry Centre, Batsford Park.

At the bottom of Bourton's hill, still on the A44, a left turn leads to the **Batsford Arboretum** and the **Cotswold Falconry Centre** in Batsford Park. The arboretum was the work of Lord Redesdale, a diplomat at the British Embassy in Tokyo, who brought back cherry trees, magnolia and Japanese maples on his return to the Cotswolds. Redesdale was also responsible for the mansion, despite its Elizabethan styling. Over the last thirty years the arboretum has been greatly expanded (it is now one of Britain's largest private arboreta), though the emphasis is still on magnolias and larch, and enhanced: a visit in spring when the daffodils are in bloom is especially worthwhile. Dotted around the park are bronzes which Lord Redesdale also brought back from Japan, these including a marvellous Buddha. The arboretum includes a garden centre with plants, aquatic items, tools and machinery. The Falconry Centre has around seventy birds of prey including eagles, falcons and owls. There are breeding aviaries and regular displays of flying.

At the north-eastern edge of Batsford Park is the small estate village of Batsford where the memorial tablet in the church to Thomas Freeman, who died in 1089, is well worth seeing. The tablet, in coloured marble, was the work of the sculptor Joseph Nollekens.

Sezincote.

The visit to Batsford Park was a short detour on our route. To continue, take the minor road heading south from Bourton-on-the-Hill to reach **Sezincote**, one of the most extraordinary places in the Cotswolds. Sir Charles Cockerell had made a fortune working for the East India Company and returned to Britain determined to live the life of a country gentleman in style. He therefore enlisted his brother Samuel Pepys Cockerell, an architect with the East India Company, and the Indian topographical artist Thomas Daniell to help to create a patch of local oriental splendour. Sezincote had been a village at the time of the Domesday Book, but had lost its church and most of its houses to sheep grazing. The old manorial house did exist, however, and in 1805 this was converted into what we see today, a house of oriental details, but retaining the requirements necessary to combat the British climate – note that beside the onion dome there are chimney stacks. The dome is interesting because it is the most obvious feature linking the house to Mogul, rather than Hindu, India. Indeed, Sezincote is one of few buildings in Europe which are identifiably Mogul: the already honey-coloured stone was stained to copy more exactly the orange of Mogul Asia, and some windows are peacock-tailed. The dome was of burnished copper, but now carries a patina of age. Inside, the Indian theme was dropped in favour of a classical design, though there was still an eccentricity: the sumptuous reception rooms are on the first floor, with Sir Charles's living rooms being at ground level.

For the park surrounding the house the ideas of Thomas Daniell were combined with those of Humphrey Repton. The drive crosses an Indian bridge; the conservatory has minarets and a pavilion; there are cast-iron Brahmin bulls and Hindu goats. Around these Repton styled a water garden fed by a natural stream to contrast with the ancient woodland, though the oriental theme is maintained with clumps of bamboo and Japanese maple.

It is known that the Prince Regent visited Sezincote in 1807, and it is almost certainly the case that the extraordinary nature of the house influenced his decision for the design of the Brighton Pavilion.

Sir Charles Cockerell died in 1837 and was buried in a tomb in the church at **Longborough**, a beautiful village nicely sited on a hillside to the south of the park. Here, at least, Sir Charles is outdone – the tomb of Sir William Leigh, who died two centuries earlier, being far more elaborate. On it Sir William lies in effigy, accompanied by his wife and children.

Now turn off the A424 towards Condicote, the road dropping steeply then climbing again as the village is approached. Condicote lies just off the line of Ryknield Street, a Roman road that ran from the Fosse Way near Bourton-on-the-Water northwards to Sheffield. To the south of the village the Street, still a well-defined track, offers a splendid walk to the high point of the local wolds, a round trip of no more than 4km (2½ miles) but one offering superb views of the high wold country. Turn left on entering the village, then left again at the T-junction to reach the Donnington Trout Farm where fly-fishing on a lake stocked with rainbow and brown trout is possible all year around, and fresh and smoked trout may be bought. On the far end of the same lake is the Donnington Brewery, where 'real ale' is still brewed. The Brewery is not open to the public, but its ale may be sampled in many local inns – look for the black and white Donnington sign.

From Condicote head south to the B4077 and turn right towards Temple Guiting. Ignore the first crossroads, but turn left at the second to reach the **Cotswold Farm Park**. The Park is an Approved Centre of the Rare Breeds Survival Trust and has about fifty breeding herds and flocks of old British breeds of sheep, horses, cattle, pigs and poultry. A new addition to the Park's attraction is the Touch Barn where children may touch or handle some of the breeds and a range of traditional pets. There is also an adventure playground, a viewing tower and a nature trail through the farmland.

Continue along the B4077 to reach the turning on the left for Temple Guiting. Our tour goes that way, but first makes a short detour to visit Snowshill Manor. Continue along the B4077, going through Ford, a delightful little hamlet whose inn has an inviting little verse above the door. North of Ford, beyond Cutsdean and Teddington, near Field Barn, is the source of the Windrush, the most 'Cotswold' of all the area's rivers. Ford is so-named because here the infant Windrush could be forded.

Further along the B4077 is Stumps Cross, the stump being of a medieval cross that once marked the crossroads. Turn right at the crossroads, following a minor road to Snowshill. The village, which can be easily reached from Broadway by following the

A Shirehorse ride, Cotswold Farm Park.

road past the old church, is usually visited for its Manor, and, while this is understandable, the virtues of the rest of the village are thereby excluded. Snowshill is beautifully sited, with views out across the Vale of Evesham. The village cottages try to group themselves around the green and the little church (Norman, but rebuilt in the mid-nineteenth century), but fail, drifting down the hillside towards Buckland Wood. But though the site gives panoramic views, it is also exposed: Snowshill is rightly

Snowshill Manor.

named: if snow falls on the Cotswolds it stays longer here than elsewhere, and winter's winds blow harder and colder.

Snowshill Manor is an early sixteenth-century house (though remodelled later) of local stone, solid rather than elegant, built, it seems, to withstand nature's battering. It acquired minor infamy in 1604 when Anne Parsons, a fifteen-year-old girl staying in the village, eloped and was married at the house. Anne was heiress to a considerable fortune following the death of her mother, whose will placed her into the guardianship of her tutor, stipulating that she live at the Snowshill house of the will's executor. It seems likely that the executor, perhaps even the tutor, had designs on Anne, probably wishing to marry her to acquire the fortune. On the eve of St. Valentine's Day, Anthony Palmer, her former boyfriend (lover?), from Elmley Castle near Bredon Hill, arrived late at night with a small armed gang. Anne was taken to the Manor and married Anthony there in a service performed by the vicar of Broadway church. Although the elopement (or abduction if you prefer the tutor's view) was a sensation at the time, history does not record how the couple fared. However, since Anne's ghost is said to haunt the Manor, it must be assumed to have been an unhappy match.

Snowshill Manor is now famous for the collection of Charles Paget Wade. Wade, a Suffolk man, had made a fortune in the West Indies and bought the Manor in 1919. It was in a poor state of repair; Wade restored it in good style and then filled it with what could be best described as a 'magpie collection' of curios. There are old craft tools and farm implements, musical instruments (including two serpents), clocks, toys and dolls, old bicycles (a superb collection) and much else besides. There is also a collection of Japanese samurai armour, the finest in Britain. The collection attracted many famous visitors – Edwin Lutyens, John Buchan, John Masefield, J.B. Priestley and Queen Mary (who maintained that the best item in the house was Wade himself). One interesting, minor detail is that Wade did not actually live in the Manor, preferring to stay in the nearby Priest's House. In 1951 he gave the Manor and its collection to the National Trust and returned to the

Snowshill Manor.

West Indies. He came back to Snowshill for a visit in 1956, was taken ill at Broadway and died in Evesham Hospital. He is buried in Snowshill churchyard. Today the National Trust maintains the Manor and collection much as it was when Wade left it. The collection is the most remarkable in the Cotswolds, but the large garden and grounds surrounding the Manor are also worth exploring. There is a restaurant from the terrace of which the view westwards is magnificent.

Temple Guiting acquired its prefix when it was owned, in the twelfth century, by the Knights Templar who wished to distinguish it from the second Guiting village to the south. The second part of the name is from the same route as 'gushing', the Windrush being more imposing here than at nearby Ford. To the south-west of the village is Guiting Wood, an excellent piece of ancient woodland crossed by a narrow, unforgiving road and several good walking paths.

Our route now follows the Windrush southwards. Somewhere near here was the settlement of *Cod*, the Saxon whose upland farm – Cod's Wold – has named the area. Go through Kineton, where the Windrush was again once forded, and the hamlet of Burton, where the Windrush forms a pool, to reach a right turn for **Guiting Power**. Here the village houses cluster around a green on which stands a war memorial in the form of a medieval cross. The village church, which has a magnificent Norman doorway, houses a stone coffin obviously made for a child, a sad relic.

Back on the road through the Windrush valley, head southwards to reach a right turn to **Naunton**. The village began as a hamlet in a hollow of the valley, but has since grown and, confined by the valley slopes, spread out along a single street. It is, perhaps, the one village in the Cotswolds that looks much better from a distance – for instance, from the B4068 that runs to the south and above the village. Yet there are things of interest here. At the western end is a four-gabled dovecote constructed in the late sixteenth century, carefully restored about fifty years ago but now in need of further restoration. The dovecote looks so much like a house, that many visitors pass it without ever realizing its real purpose. In the village church look for the memorial tablet to Ambrose Oldys, the son of Dr William Oldys, the vicar of Adderbury in Oxfordshire. The tablet notes the cleric's Royalist sympathies during the Civil War and his death in 1645, when he was 'barbarously murthered by ye rebels'. The tablet notes the death of Ambrose himself (in 1710) almost as an after-thought.

The medieval dovecote, Naunton.

The B4068 offers a quick return to Cheltenham, but the better return is by way of a series of small wold villages. Go back to the crossroads on the B4068 and turn along the minor road through the hamlet of Aylworth to reach the A436. To the right from here (about 2km, 1¼ miles, and on the southern – left-hand – side of the road) is the Notgrove long barrow. The excavated finds from this large but not too well preserved site are in the Cheltenham Town Museum. **Notgrove**, to the south of the A436, is also grouped around a green. The church has a Saxon crucifix (eroded and in primitive style, but very rare) in a niche on its east wall. Inside there are memorials to members of the Whittington family, descendants of Sir Richard, the Dick Whittington of cat and pantomime fame. East of the village and reached from the A436 (turn left instead of right for the village when approaching from Aylworth) is **Folly Farm**, dedicated to the breeding of rare waterfowl and poultry, with over 150 different species of ducks, geese, chickens and wildfowl. Children will be enthralled by the incubator shed where young chicks are reared. In addition to the birds there are deer, goats and rabbits, and a pets area. The farm also has a nursery with rare species of trees and shrubs for sale.

To the east of Notgrove, named, it is said, for the hazel trees that once surrounded the village, is **Cold Aston**, named for its exposed position on the high wolds. There was a move a hundred years ago to change the village's name to Aston Blank to avoid confusion with Cold Ashton in the Southwolds. Not surprisingly the change was viewed without enthusiasm by the residents, though the alternative name still exists on some signposts, to the confusion of unwary visitors. Here, too, there is a green, with a large sycamore tree that has given its name to Sycamore House, a fine Georgian building.

To the south of Notgrove is **Turkdean** – also reached by a bridleway from Cold Aston, one offering an exceptional walk across the high wolds. The village is divided into two hamlets linked by a road through an area of fine beech trees. Head south-eastwards to reach the A429 (Fosse Way), turning right to its roundabout junction with the A40 outside Northleach. Go right here, soon turning left to **Hampnett**, a scattered village around a large green. Close to the village is the source of the River Leach, after the Windrush the most famous and attractive of Cotswold rivers, which runs eastwards to join the Thames on the Oxfordshire border.

Continue along the A40 towards Cheltenham, soon passing a road to the right for **Hazleton**, a secluded little village thought to lie on the salt route across the high wolds. To the north, in **Salperton** church was a medieval wall painting of a skeleton holding a scythe and an arrow, perhaps an early rendering of Father Time, and a warning to the congregation that death comes to everyone. Salperton Park, beside the church, is an elegant mansion. Part of it is seventeenth-century, though it was extended and altered in about 1817.

Continue along the A40 to its junction with the A436 (to the left). A left turn here leads quickly to the Kilkenny viewpoint from where the high wolds may be viewed. At the same junction a right turn follows a minor road into the villages of

Shipton Solers and **Shipton Oliffe**. The church at Solers (occasionally spelt as Sollers) has a stained glass window with a ship as the central motif. It is believed that the artist misunderstood the meaning of the first part of the village's name, which derives from sheep, not ship. Look, too, for the hour-glass by the pulpit, presumably used by the vicar to ensure he did not bore the congregation with long sermons. Both villages lie prettily on a tributary of the River Coln.

There is another A40/A436 junction at **Andoversford**, though the village, a straggling, undistinguished place, is bypassed. Continue along the A40 to reach a turn to the right for **Whittington**, noteworthy for Whittington Court, a multi-gabled manor house. The Court was begun in the sixteenth century by Robert Cotton, whose memorial brass (together with his wife) may be seen in the church. Cotton did not finish the building, being killed in a duel in 1556. The Court stands on the site of an earlier, moated manor house, and was extended in the eighteenth and the early twentieth century. The original Court was visited by Elizabeth I on 9 September 1592: she dined here before moving on to Sudeley Castle for three days of celebrations to mark the anniversary of the defeat of the Spanish Armada.

The road to Whittington continues to Syreford and on to Sevenhampton and Brockhampton, the former with a good wool church endowed by John Comber, a wool merchant whose memorial brass may be seen inside, the latter with a fine manor house.

Back on the A40, we now descend into Cheltenham. To the left is the village of Dowdeswell, split into Upper and Lower halves as it climbs the Cotswold Edge. The church, in the lower village, is cruciform. It has high-pitched roofs and a similarly pointed porch. Together with the pyramidal tower this collection of gables gives it a very pleasing outline when viewed across the churchyard. Across the main road from the village is Dowdeswell Reservoir, the last landmark before Cheltenham is entered through the suburb village of Charlton Kings.

Whittington Court
and church.

ADDRESSES AND OPENING TIMES

SLEEPY HOLLOW FARM PARK,
Draycott Road, Blockley *(01386 701264)*
❖
OPEN: Easter–early Nov, daily, 10.00am–6.00pm
(last entry at 5.00pm)

ARBORETUM,
Batsford Park *(01608 650722)*
❖
OPEN: March–early Nov, daily, 10.00am–5.00pm;
the Garden Centre is open all year, same times
(01386 700409)

COTSWOLD FALCONRY CENTRE,
Batsford Park *(01386 701043)*
❖
OPEN: March–early Nov, daily, 10.00am–5.00pm

SEZINCOTE,
near Bourton-on-the-Hill *(01386 700444)*

❖

OPEN: house, May–July and Sept, Thurs and Fri, 2.30–5.30pm;
garden, all year except Dec, Thurs, Fri
and Bank Holiday Mon, 2.00–6.00pm or dusk

DONNINGTON TROUT FARM,
near Condicote *(0141 830873)*

❖

OPEN: April–Oct, daily, 10.00am–5.30pm;
Nov–March, daily except Mon, 10.00am–5.00pm

COTSWOLD FARM PARK,
near Temple Guiting *(01451 850307)*

❖

OPEN: Easter–Sept, daily, 10.00am–5.00pm
(6.00pm in July and Aug and Bank Holiday Mon)

SNOWSHILL MANOR,
Snowshill *(01386 852410)*

❖

OPEN: Easter–Oct, daily except Tues, 1.00–5.00pm;
garden open July and Aug, Tues, from 12.00pm

FOLLY FARM,
near Notgrove *(01451 820285)*

❖

OPEN: May–Sept, daily, 10.00am–6.00pm;
Oct–April, daily, 10.00am–3.30pm
(shop open until 5.00pm)

WHITTINGTON COURT,
Whittington

❖

OPEN: Easter Sat and following 15 days and 127 days
before and including Aug Bank Holiday, 2.00–5.00pm

(Opposite) The Market Square, Cirencester.

Cheltenham
and the
Roman Cotswolds

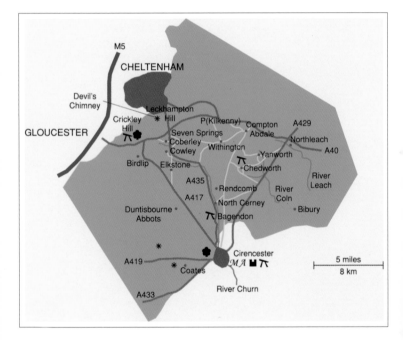

It is possible that the Romans were the first to introduce the famous Cotswold sheep – the Cotswold Lion – to the area. It is certainly true that the area was important to them: Roman Cirencester was a major town and the area was crossed by equally important roads. Here, too, at Chedworth, the most important Roman villa so far excavated has been discovered. This tour visits the significant Roman sites and more besides.

TOUR 3: Cheltenham to Cirencester

Leave Cheltenham along the A435 towards Cirencester, climbing to the road's off-set junction with the A436. To the right here, a short distance from the crossroads and on the right, is **Seven Springs**, argued by many to be the true source of the River Thames. The acknowledged source is at Thameshead, further south, where the River Churn, a tributary, rises. It is a moot point, however, as Seven Springs is further from Westminster, say, than Thameshead. It has to be agreed though that Thameshead is a more imposing site: at Seven Springs the Churn emerges from a muddy pool at the base of a stone wall, in a hollow beside a lay-by of the main road. Continue along the A435, soon turning right to reach **Coberley**, where the village church is reached through the arched doorway of a farm. This looks extremely unlikely despite the signpost, but is quite correct regardless of the sense of intrusion that the visitor might feel. The first church here was probably Saxon, and there was certainly a Norman building before the present one was built in about 1340. Inside there are a number of interesting memorials. Look first for that of Sir Giles Berkeley in the sanctuary. The tiny effigy of a knight in mail (Sir Giles himself?) clutches a heart. This is a heart burial, the only one of its kind in the Cotswolds. The body of Sir Giles lies at Little Malvern. Such separate internments (occasionally involving more than two 'pieces' of the deceased) were common at the time, when the Norman

Sir Giles Berkeley's Heart Burial, Coberley.

knights held estates in different parts of the country. Even rarer than the heart burial is the burial of Sir Giles's favourite horse Lombard in the churchyard, animals being buried in consecrated ground only when the lord of the manor was formidable enough to give the priest no choice. It is believed that Lombard lies under the mound to the north of the church rather than below the new memorial tablet on the other side of the wall from the heart burial.

Also in the church is the tomb of Sir Thomas Berkeley, who lies in effigy on it, together with his wife. Sir Thomas was instrumental in raising the army that defeated the rebellion against Edward II at Boroughbridge in 1322. As a result, the King made him responsible for the recruitment of archers. Sir Thomas held this responsibility under Edward III too, and men he had recruited, some from the Cotswolds, helped to win the Battle of Crecy in 1346, where Sir Thomas also fought. Following his death (in around 1355), his wife Joan married Sir William Whittington. They had a son Richard (later Sir Richard) who famously turned again, becoming Lord Mayor of London three times. He must be the most unlikely pantomime character of them all.

Further along the A435 a right turn leads to **Cowley**, a sheltered village with a fine manor house, built in 1855 in Italianate style with a series of terraces down which the River

Churn formed cascades. The manor is now an educational centre for the county council. Lewis Carroll is reputed to have conceived the idea for *Alice in Wonderland* while staying at Cowley's Rectory. The next right turn leads to **Elkstone**, where the church is not only the highest in the Cotswolds but the most perfectly preserved Norman building, with some outstanding architectural features. The south doorway has a tympanum (the semi-circular slab above a doorway) carved with a Christ in Majesty together with the symbols of the Evangelists, above which is an arch of carved beakheads (monsters and birds, but including two human heads). Inside there is a corbel table, the corbels carved with animals, birds and zodiacal signs, and a magnificent chancel arch with a carved chevron mould. Even rarer than these features is the columbarium or pigeon loft, above the chancel, reached by a stairway near the pulpit. This is a reminder of the time when pigeons and pigeon eggs were an important source of food.

The A435 follows the valley of the Churn from the Elkstone turn, a wooded valley of great beauty. The road touches the edge of **Colesbourne**, but a turn (to the left) is required to visit

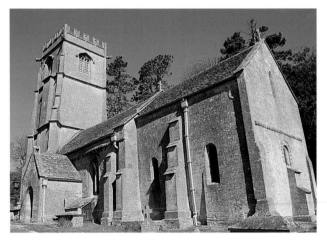

Elkstone Church.

the church which has a rare stone pulpit. The church is at the edge of Colesbourne Park, planted by Henry Elwes, who died in 1922. Elwes was a great traveller and brought back many rare trees for his park.

Beyond Colesbourne, turn left along a narrow, steep lane that runs beside Colesbourne Park, then bears right across high wold before descending to **Withington** in the valley of the River Coln. The church here has a beautifully sculpted memorial to Sir John Howe and his wife, including both the couple and their eight children, though its position, high on the south-west wall, means that it is difficult to appreciate. From Withington take the road for Compton Abdale climbing to the high wold then descending equally steeply. **Compton Abdale** is a wonderful hamlet, set beside a little stream that springs from stones seemingly placed

The 'Crocodile' Spring, Compton Abdale.

to create the mouth of a crocodile, by the churchyard. The village is another of those on the ancient salt way across the Cotswolds, the way coming from Droitwich, the salt being used to cure meat for winter eating. The village church, dedicated to St. Oswald – as the village was once owned by St. Oswald's Priory in Gloucester – has lovely gargoyles.

From Compton Abdale head south along a road that descends to the River Coln, before rising through beautiful woodland. After crossing the Coln, turn left along the woodland edge to reach **Chedworth Roman Villa**. The villa was discovered in 1864 by a gamekeeper who noticed *tesserae* (the coloured stones from which mosaics are made) being thrown out of a warren by burrowing rabbits. Excavations revealed the remains of a villa with thirty-two rooms, now regarded as the finest in Britain. The rooms were arranged around two courtyards, the outer one at a lower level than the other. The villa had two baths, one for dry heat and one for steam (what we would now call a sauna and a Turkish bath). The hypocaust – the under-floor heating system, with the floor mounted on columns creating a honeycomb through which hot air circulated – can be seen, as can also the remains of several mosaics, the unques-tioned highlight of the site. That in the west wing includes a repre-sentation of the four seasons in the four cor-ners: summer depicted as a well-fed figure of plenty, a sharp contrast to winter, which is a cloak-shrouded figure

Chedworth Roman Villa.

clutching a hare for the evening meal and a branch for the fire. The site (now in the hands of the National Trust) also has a vis-itor centre where a short, but excellent video gives an introduc-tion to the site, and a museum with the best of the excavated finds. Today the villa stands among the trees of Chedworth Wood, which enhances its appearance, but it is thought that at the time it was inhabited it stood on open wold. As an interesting aside, the damp parts of the surrounding woodland are now home to edible snails, presumably imported by the villa's owners who wanted a taste of mainland Europe.

To reach the village of Chedworth either continue along the road from the villa site to reach Yanworth or return to the road from Compton Abdale. Yanworth is little more than a hamlet, but a very pleasant one on the hillside above the Coln. The little Norman church has a medieval wall painting of a skeleton with a scythe, presumably Father Time.

Approaching Chedworth from the Coln and crossing to the south of Compton Abdale, the visitor climbs through beautiful woodland to arrive, bizarrely, on a disused airfield. Follow the road across it and then descend into **Chedworth**, a straggling village clinging to both sides of the tight valley of a tributary stream of the Coln. It is best seen not from our approach, but from the descent of Pancake Hill, on the eastern side of the village (and reached from Fossebridge on the A429). Despite its hilly nature, Chedworth was once bisected by a railway, its creation a monument to the engineers' skill. The prettiest part of the village is at the western end, near the Seven Tuns Inn and the church; the spring jumping from the wall opposite the inn adds to the quaintness. St. Andrew's Church is late Norman and has a carved stone pulpit. The wall above the northern arcades has one corbel carved with the head of Henry VII's Queen (Elizabeth of York) who visited the manor. It is not clear whether she would have stayed at the present Manor House; though this has definite medieval features it was extensively altered in the seventeenth century.

From Chedworth head south along a road that is arrow-straight across North Cerney Downs: again you are following the Cotswold salt way. The village of **North Cerney** is reached by turning right. Go through the village to reach the A435. The church, opposite, has been beautifully restored and is probably now much the way it looked before the Puritans cleared out what they considered idolatrous. There is a medieval stone altar and what many experts consider to be the finest stone pulpit in the Cotswolds. The rood screen still supports a sculpture of Christ, one believed to have been carved in Italy around 1600. The church also has two carvings on its outer walls, probably the work of stone masons employed to restore the church after a fire in the late sixteenth century. On the south wall of the south transept is a *man-*

The manticore *carved on the outer wall of North Cerney Church.*

ticore, a beast with the head of a man and the body of a lion, while on the south-west buttress there is a leopard.

North Cerney House, up the hill from the church, is a fine Georgian house whose gardens and woods are open to visitors. The walled garden has roses and herbs, while the woodland is especially good in late spring when the bluebells are in bloom.

To the right from North Cerney, along a winding section of the main road, is **Rendcomb**. Here the church has a marvellous Norman tub-font, carved with eleven Apostles and a blank where Judas would have stood. Nearby Rendcomb College was built in the 1860s by Sir Francis Goldsmid. A curious fact is that the towers on the fine Italianate building and the stables were built so that Sir Francis could watch the growth of trees he had planted in groups such that they spelt his name in Hebrew.

Now head along the A435 towards Cirencester, soon passing a turn on the right for **Bagendon** where there are huge earthworks, probably dating from the Iron Age. The site, enclosed by the ditches and the sharp valley slope, is almost 80ha (200 acres) in area, leading to speculation that Bagendon was the site of a tribal capital.

Continue along the A435, reaching the A417 at Baunton. Turn left to reach Cirencester.

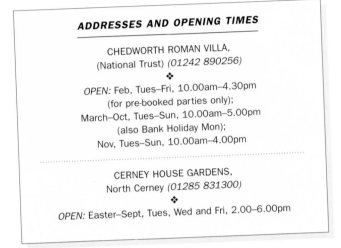

ADDRESSES AND OPENING TIMES

CHEDWORTH ROMAN VILLA,
(National Trust) *(01242 890256)*
❖
OPEN: Feb, Tues–Fri, 10.00am–4.30pm
(for pre-booked parties only);
March–Oct, Tues–Sun, 10.00am–5.00pm
(also Bank Holiday Mon);
Nov, Tues–Sun, 10.00am–4.00pm

CERNEY HOUSE GARDENS,
North Cerney *(01285 831300)*
❖
OPEN: Easter–Sept, Tues, Wed and Fri, 2.00–6.00pm

Cirencester

When the Romans invaded Britain in AD43 they moved rapidly westwards, meeting resistance that was occasionally stubborn and bloody, but more frequently token. When the Romans arrived there seems to have been little resistance in the area around what is now Cirencester and no organized settlement at the site beside the River Churn; but there was the large site at Bagendon, a little way to the north. It is conjectured that this was the tribal capital of the Dobunni Celts, under the rule of King Boduocus. Despite the minimal resistance on their arrival the Romans would have been anxious to keep an eye on the Bagendon site and, perhaps not wishing to evict too many folk (as a conciliatory gesture) or, more likely, not wishing to be too close in case of trouble, the Romans chose Cirencester as the site of a fort, calling it Corinium. Because of its position at the extreme western end of their new kingdom, Corinium rapidly became important, and more so when the great roads of Fosse Way, Ermin Street and Akeman Street met at the fort.

In time, the border of Roman Britain moved further west and Corinium lost its status as a frontier garrison town. But the important crossroads meant that it became increasingly prosperous as a market town. Soon it was the second largest town after London in the new province. The subsequent destruction of the town by the Saxons and overbuilding in later centuries means that little of Corinium now remains above ground. In Abbey Grounds there is a restored section of the town wall and the line of the wall is followed by an earth bank. Rather more impressive is Corinium's amphitheatre (reached from Cotswold Avenue, to the south of the ring road), one of the best preserved in Britain. This is an oval surrounded by a bank of rubble that would originally have been retained by a stone wall.

Although the visible remains of Roman Cirencester are limited, the excavated remains are magnificent, forming a collection in the Corinium Museum in Park Street that is one of the finest in Britain and one of the best presented. These are so complete that they have allowed Roman life to be reconstructed in excellent tableaux. The finds indicate that in addition to private villas, Corinium was well-stocked with shops and craftsmen and all the other necessities of civilized Roman life. There were doctors as well, including one who specialized in eye complaints: the instructions for the use of one of his ointments survive: 'Atticus's Frankincense Salve. For all pains – to be made up with an egg'.

Such items exploring the ordinariness of Roman life are a fascinating insight into the period, but most visitors will be most entranced by the excavated mosaics. Corinium was clearly a rich town, its wealthy merchants and officials able to afford the luxuries of Roman life – baths, hypocausts to relieve the miseries of a northern European winter, and fine mosaics. The specimens on display, and the illustrations of how they would have looked when complete, indicate that the mosaic artists of the town were of the highest ability. Though pride of place goes to the famous 'Hare Mosaic', with its central motif of a Cotswold hare, look for the details in some of the others, for instance, the winged sea serpent excavated from Dyer Street.

One other item must also be mentioned, the famous word square found in Victoria Road in 1868. The square, forming the words *Rotas Opera Tenet Arepo Sator* which reads both up and down and left and right, forms an apparently meaningless sentence ('The sower Arepo holds the wheel carefully'). It could be, of course, that the meaning was not as important as the cleverness of the design, but it has been noticed that rearranged the letters form a cross reading *Paternoster* on both the upright and the crosspiece, with the letters A and O (alpha and omega?) remaining. It is therefore conjectured that the square (incised on an irregular fragment of wall plaster) is an early Christian symbol, produced when Christianity had reached Britain, but was still outlawed by the Roman state.

The museum also includes a recreation of the garden of a Roman town house and exhibitions on other periods of Cirencester's past, both before and after the Roman occupation.

Following the departure of the Romans from Britain, Corinium was eventually occupied by the Saxons, who wrested it from its Romano-British occupiers during their relentless push westwards. The Saxons did not occupy towns such as Cirencester, preferring smaller settlements and having a less luxurious lifestyle. Corinium was destroyed, perhaps gradually as the buildings decayed or the stone was used for other purposes. There was certainly a Saxon church, but it is not until the arrival of the Normans that Cirencester is seen again with certainty. In the early years of the twelfth century a huge Augustinian abbey was built in the town, its wealth bringing prosperity for 400 years until its dissolution. Now all that remains of St. Mary's Abbey is the name of the Abbey Gardens and the nearby Spital Gate, the Abbey's gateway.

The loss of the Abbey was not as devastating for the town as similar losses elsewhere – Cirencester was already a market town, and the Cotswold woollen industry had made it extremely prosperous. As a large and important market town it survived the collapse of the wool trade, and has remained a vibrant place since.

An exploration of Cirencester has to start at the Church of St. John the Baptist. The church, the largest parish church in Gloucestershire, is one of the trio of great Cotswold wool churches (with Chipping Campden and Northleach). It is a church of superlatives – the tallest tower in Gloucestershire at just over 49m (162ft), the oldest twelve-bell peel in England, the largest porch of any English church. The bells are rung on 29 May to celebrate the Restoration, and a 'Pancake Bell' is rung on Shrove Tuesday, both these now being rare ringings in Britain. St. John's is a breathtakingly beautiful building, the porch, which fronts the Market Place, being a fitting entry into a spacious interior every bit as fine as the exterior. The first church on the site was built in the early twelfth century, with additions through to 1400 when the tower was added. Later, in about 1520, the nave was virtually demolished, the great Tudor nave being built. The south porch was built in 1490 on land that

belonged to the Abbey rather than the town. It is almost a separate building and was indeed separate after its construction, forming the Abbot's offices. After the dissolution the porch became the Town Hall, being given to the church only in the seventeenth century. It is, almost without question, the finest church porch in England and stands three storeys high and three bays

Cirencester Church Porch.

wide and deep, with a superb open stonework parapet and ground-floor ceiling vaulting.

Inside the church there is one of the few pre-Reformation wine-glass pulpits in the country, a fine stone piece with good tracery. There are also some remarkable brass memorials. That of William Prelatte, who died in 1462, shows him in full armour and flanked by his two wives. Prelatte was a wool merchant who gave money to the church. The brass of Reginald Spycer, another wool merchant, who died in 1442, has him with his four wives, while that of Robert Pope, also a wool merchant, who died in 1434, shows his wife, six sons and eight daughters. Look, too, for the late fifteenth-century wall paintings in St. Catherine's Chapel, on either side of the altar. The smaller murals at the western end of the chapel's north wall are at least a century older. While you are in the chapel, look upwards at the splendid stone fan-vaulting. Finally, the church plate is considered to be one of the most interesting collections in England and is well worth some time examining. Taking pride of place is the Boleyn Cup. The gilded silver cup is hallmarked 1535 and bears the crest of the family of Anne Boleyn. The pair of jug-shaped flagons, dated 1576, are very rare and the finest of their type in Britain.

Unfortunately, for insurance reasons the tower is now infrequently open to visitors. If it is, be sure to take the opportunity of an excellent view of the town and of Cirencester Park to the west. The mansion was built in the early eighteenth century for the first Earl Bathurst, the patron of Alexander Pope. It is famously told that after it had been completed the Earl asked Pope, 'How comes it to look so oddly bad?' He was correct: despite the attempt at architectural wholeness the building was not a success, though doubtless that is not the reason it is hidden from the town by one of the largest yew hedges in the world. The huge Park behind the house was much more successful, though the plan, with straight rides radiating from a central point, would soon be made to look old-fashioned by Capability Brown's naturalism. Although it is private, the Park is open to walkers and riders, though access to the polo ground favoured by royalty is controlled. Dotted around the park are a number of follies: Alfred's Hall, built in 1721, is one of the earliest such buildings in the country. Another, Pope's Seat, is named for Alexander Pope. The Park is entered from Cecily Hill.

On the other side of the Market Place from the church is the nineteenth-century Corn Hall which now houses the Tourist Information Office, while close to the Market Place, in Brewery Court at the elbow of Castle Street and Cricklade Street, is the Brewery Arts Centre in which there are twelve independent craft shops.

To the north of the church lie the best preserved streets from Cirencester's prosperous wool-trade era. Go along Godsditch Street /Dollar Street on the west side of the church, passing the town's medieval High Cross. Dollar Street is named for the Dole Hall (almonry) of the Abbey. To the left is Coxwell Street. As in Dollar Street the houses here are from the seventeenth and the eighteenth century. Coxwell Street leads to Thomas Street; bear left to reach Cecily Hill with more excellent wool merchants' houses. At the end of Cecily Hill is the entrance to Cirencester Park and, to the right, a castle-like building which was, in fact, the barracks of the Royal North Gloucestershire Militia

Coxwell Street, Cirencester.

93

The Hare Mosaic, Corinium Museum.

Armoury, built in 1857. It is now owned by a training company. Just around the corner from the entrance to Cecily Hill is Park Street and the Corinium Museum.

The next left from Dollar Street is Thomas Street. Here stands the oldest secular building in the town, St. Thomas's Hospital (also known as Weavers Hall), founded by Sir William Nottingham who died in 1483. The memorial brass to Sir William's father (also a William) is the oldest in St. John's Church. To the right from Dollar Street, almost opposite Thomas Street, is Spitalgate Lane with another almshouse – St. John's Hospital, founded by Henry II – to the left. A section of the Norman arcading of the original building remains, though the almshouses were rebuilt in 1826. From the lane the Abbey's Spital Gate can be reached, giving access to the Abbey Grounds and a beautiful walk beside the River Churn.

Back in the town the pedestrian precinct of Cricklade

The Abbey Grounds, Cirencester.

Street, together with Castle Street, Market Place and Dyer Street, offer the best of Cirencester's shops. In Dyer Street the Bear Inn, a seventeenth-century, half-timbered building with three storeys and two overhangs, is delightful.

Finally, head to the southern part of the town where, in Trinity Road, is the Cirencester Lock-Up, one of the few remaining such in Britain and one of the even fewer that are open to the public. The lock-up was built in 1804 (before there were police stations) on a different site, and moved here in 1837 to form part of the town's workhouse (which now houses the offices of the Cotswold District Council). With its curiously half-cylindrical roof it is an interesting little building.

ADDRESSES AND OPENING TIMES

CORINIUM MUSEUM,
Park Street *(01285 655611)*
❖
OPEN: April–Oct, Mon–Sat, 10.00am–5.00pm,
Sun 2.00–5.00pm;
Nov–March, Tues–Sat, 10.00am–5.00pm,
Sun 2.00–5.00pm;
Bank Holidays apart from Christmas Day and Boxing Day

BREWERY ARTS,
Brewery Court *(01285 657181)*
❖
OPEN: all year, Mon–Sat, 10.00am–5.00pm;
closed Bank Holidays

CIRENCESTER LOCK-UP,
Trinity Road *(01285 655611)*
❖
OPEN: all year, Mon–Fri, 9.00am–5.00pm; at other times
the key may be obtained from the Corinium Museum

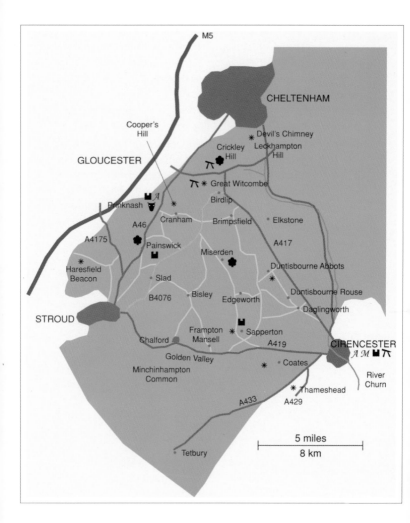

TOUR 4: Cirencester to Cheltenham:
the Hidden Cotswolds

Our return to Cheltenham explores a 'secret' part of the Cotswold, visiting delightful villages hidden among the folds of the tight valleys. Beyond these villages it continues through one of the finest towns in the area.

Take the Cirencester ring road as far as the roundabout on the western side of the town, bearing right there along the A419 towards Stroud. This road runs beside Cirencester Park, the Overley Ride – leading to the focal point of the rides (called, somewhat prosaically, Ten Rides) – soon being seen on the right. Just beyond, turn right for Sapperton.

Sapperton is an interesting little village, with a place in both the industrial and artistic heritage of the Cotswolds. In the churchyard of St. Kenelm's Church lie Ernest Gimson and the Barnsley brothers, Ernest and Sidney, the architects and furniture makers who were significant members of William Morris's Arts and Crafts Movement. The three moved into nearby Daneway House in the 1890s and worked there until their deaths (Gimson in 1917, both the Barnsleys in 1926).

Inside the church is an excellent memorial to Sir Henry Poole who died in 1616. He is shown kneeling with his wife, the pair surrounded by their children. Poole was a native of Sapperton, as was Charles Mason, born in the village in 1728. Mason was at one time the assistant to James Bradley, the Astronomer Royal, then emigrated to the American Colonies where, with Jeremiah Dixon, he surveyed the disputed boundary between Pennsylvania and Maryland. The subsequent extension of this line, the Mason-Dixon Line, came to be considered as the boundary between the slave and the free states.

From the church, take the path heading downhill to visit the entrance to the Sapperton canal tunnel. The canal was the Thames and Severn, opened in 1789 to link the Stroudwater Canal (and, therefore, the Severn) to the Thames near Lechlade.

The tunnel was a remarkable feat of engineering. It took almost six years to bore its 3.5km (3,817yd) and was the longest in Britain at the time of its construction. Sadly the effort was almost in vain. The canal suffered a constant, usually severe, water shortage and was barely profitable even before the coming of the railways. By the early years of this century the canal had closed, the tunnel collapsing soon after. There is little hope of its ever being reopened, but the portals (here and at Coates) are delightful. The nearby Daneway Inn was built specifically for bargees on the canal: presumably they were glad of the rest and refreshment, barges being taken through the canal by 'legging' the bargee lying on his back on the barge top and 'walking' along the canal roof. Beyond the inn is Daneway House, its oldest parts dating from the late thirteenth century. It was here that Gimson and the Barnsleys worked. Until recently the House was occasionally open to the public, but is closed at present. The steep hillside behind the inn and the House is known as Daneway Banks. It is a Gloucestershire Wildlife Trust reserve, protected for its orchids.

From Sapperton, cross the canal by the Daneway Inn. The road to the right here heads north towards Edgeworth, while the left branch leads to the villages of Oakridge, Frampton Mansell and Chalford, in Stroud's Golden Valley, and the hilltop village of Bisley. **Oakridge** is known locally as Little Siberia for reasons far from clear as it is well-sheltered from winter's winds. The village church is Victorian, despite its style. **Frampton Mansell**, reached from Oakridge by a steep road, has splendid views of the Golden Valley, especially from the church (Victorian, but in Norman style). **Chalford** is a distinct link with industrial Stroud and, as such, is a complete contrast to the 'purer' Cotswold village to the north. The terraced cottages are for weavers, who worked from their homes until the building of factory mills on the canal. The more impressive houses were built by the clothiers and merchants who made their fortunes from the mills. The canal wharf and a couple of old mills can still be seen.

Bisley, on the hill above Chalford is a contrasting 'Cotswold' village, although it too grew prosperous on the cloth trade.

Thomas Keble, the brother of John Keble, one of the leaders of the Oxford Movement, was the vicar here for almost fifty years from 1827 and oversaw the restoration of the village's fine thirteenth-century church. This is unique in Britain in having an external 'Poor Soul's Light; a spire-topped, hexagonal lantern. The structure dates from the thirteenth century and candles were placed in its niches when mass was said for the poor, alms being placed in the centre. A curious Bisley legend claims that the lantern stands above an old well, down which the village priest fell to his death when on a visit to a sick parishioner one dark night. The legend goes on to claim that Bisley was excommunicated for having allowed the accident and, as a result, the villagers were not allowed to bury their dead either within the village churchyard or elsewhere in the diocese of Worcester. They therefore had to carry their dead to the closest village outside the diocese – Bibury in the Coln Valley, where a section of the grave-yard is still called the Bisley Piece. Within Bisley church look inside the font: at the bottom two fish are carved into the stone in relief so as to look as though they were swimming.

Bisley.

Bisley has one last interesting architectural feature, besides the array of beautiful golden-stone houses. At the top of George Street, close to the church is the village lock-up, dated 1824. It has two grill-fronted cells under an elaborate arch. Were the cells for men and women, or was the crime rate in Bisley so low that there was never a need to detain more than two criminals?

One of Bisley's famous springs.

In the village below the church look for Bisley's seven springs, the site of one of the Cotswolds more colourful ceremonies, one reviewed by Thomas Keble. Each year on Ascension Day the wells are 'dressed' with garlands of flowers.

The narrow road from Daneway soon reaches **Edgeworth** where a stained-glass window in the church (in the north transept) is said to represent St. Thomas à Becket. The curing of a local boy's leprosy, after he had journeyed to Canterbury and kissed St. Thomas's tomb, was one of the miracles that lead to the canonizing of Becket only two years after his death. Edgeworth Manor is a fine early eighteenth-century house.

From Edgeworth the Duntisbourne villages are easily reached: head east, dropping steeply into, and then climbing steeply out of, a tight valley to reach a crossroads. Go straight over. The next turn right leads to **Daglingworth**, the final village in the Duntisbourne Valley. The Saxons favoured this well-sheltered little valley, the village churches showing a considerable amount of Saxon work (though much of it was hidden or destroyed by restorers). At Daglingworth the major Saxon survivals are the carving of the Crucifixion on the outside wall of the chancel and three small carvings inside. Of these the most moving is that of the crucified Christ with Roman soldiers on either side, one holding a spear and scourge, the other a pole and vinegar sponge. In Daglingworth's Lower End, south of the main village, in the grounds of the Manor House, is a medieval dovecote with the revolving ladder, used to gain access to the 500 nesting holes, still in place.

The road up the Duntisbourne Valley soon reaches **Duntisbourne Rouse** where the nave of St. Michael's Church is almost certainly Saxon. The small saddleback tower was added in the late sixteenth century. In the churchyard there is a fourteenth-century cross with a very long shaft. Continuing up the valley, look to the right to catch a glimpse of Nutbeam Farm, thought to have been a grange of Cirencester Abbey and certainly, in parts, fifteenth century. Beyond is **Duntisbourne Leer**, named for the abbey which owned the village. Interestingly, the abbey in question was not at nearby Cirencester, but at Lire in Normandy.

Beyond Duntisbourne Leer the road and the River Dunt coincide, making a continuous ford for some distance. Since this was clearly avoidable, it is speculated that it was created to wash the wheels of carts and the hooves of horses using the valley road, and also to act as a dip for cartwheels, the water expanding dry wheels and creating a better fit. Beyond the ford is **Duntisbourne Abbots**, once home to Dr Matthew Baillie, physician to George III during his long illness. To further confuse the ownership of the Dunt Valley villages, the abbot of the name was of St. Peter's Abbey in Gloucester. Not surprisingly the church is dedicated to St. Peter. It is a delightful, low building, even the saddleback tower being squat. An interesting feature is the lych gate which is centrally pivoted and has folding brackets to support a coffin.

Duntisbourne Abbots.

It is believed that this is a unique feature and was probably very welcome to the coffin bearers who could compose themselves before the final steps into the church. The church stands at the top of the village, which sprawls attractively down the hillside.

From Duntisbourne Abbots it is necessary to return to Edgeworth in order to continue the tour northwards. Reverse the route and turn right along the wold-top road to reach **Miserden**. Here, too, the church is mostly Saxon (though rather over-restored in 1866 when much of the original Saxon work was destroyed). There are two excellent monuments inside: that of Sir William Sandys, on which he lies in effigy beside his wife, is beautifully carved in alabaster, while that of William Kingston is even more interesting in being painted and in having, as a 'footstool' for the effigy, not a lion or dog as was usual, but a goat eating a cabbage.

A short distance from the church is Misarden Park. The spelling is correct, the Park using an 'a' rather than an 'e' for reasons lost in time. The house is Elizabethan, built for the Sandys family, of which Sir William was a member, but was extended in Renaissance style by Sir Edward Lutyens in the 1920s. The Park is a series of terraces, with yew hedge topiary, overlooking the Golden Valley. The lower terraces are planted with shrubs and

The valley east of Painswick.

flowering trees. In spring, when the trees are in blossom and the hundreds of bulbs are in flower, Misarden is an enchanting place. There is also a walled garden with roses and clematis. The gardens are open to the public, but the house is not.

From Miserden, continue north towards Whiteway, turning left before that village to reach the B4070 opposite a road which descends to Sheepscombe. To the left the main road descends through the Slad Valley, immortalized in *Cider with Rosie*, the best-selling work of Laurie Lee whose death occurred during the preparation of this book. The valley has changed little since the time described in Lee's classic tale: **Sheepscombe**, an attractive, secluded village, also features in the book.

Turn left towards Slad and Stroud, following the road as far as Bulls Cross. There turn right, going steeply downhill into the Painswick Valley, then climb equally steeply up to Painswick itself.

Painswick, more a small town than a large village, has often been described as the Jewel of the Cotswolds, a title likely to be challenged by many towns and villages further north, but one that does recognize the beauty of its Cotswold houses, even if the local grey stone is less attractive than the honey-coloured stone of the northern area. The 'Pain' derives from the name of the first Norman lord of the manor, Pain Fitzjohn. An interesting note on Painswick history is that its earliest lords were prone to violent deaths, ten of first dozen or so dying in battle, in dreadful accidents or by execution. One was murdered and one committed suicide, while another died of a heart attack when he was told he was to be released from the Tower of London. A later lord, Sir Anthony Kingston, also died violently – drowning in suspicious circumstances – which is hardly surprising as he was a man of legendary cruelty who was hated by everyone who knew him. His greatest act of cruelty involved the Mayor of Bodmin, in Cornwall, who entertained Kingston after the Painswick man had put down a rebellion for the King in 1549. The Mayor, anxious to please a man of such bloodthirsty reputation, laid on a banquet. As they were about to sit down to eat Kingston took the Mayor to one side and told him to have a gallows erected immediately as justice had to be done. The Mayor gave the orders and a good meal was enjoyed by the pair. After the feast the Mayor took Kingston to view the gallows. Kingston eyed it suspiciously and asked whether the Mayor thought it strong enough for the job. 'Oh yes', he replied, ever anxious to please. 'Good', said Kingston, 'then get up on it, it was built for you'; and the protesting Mayor was promptly hanged.

As elsewhere, Painswick's fortune was made from wool, the fast-flowing streams in the nearby steep valleys powering as many as twenty-five mills when the trade was at its height, the prosperity allowing the building of elegant houses and one of the Cotswolds' most distinctive churches. There was a Norman church here, but this was rebuilt in the fourteenth century. The tower was built in 1430 and the spire added in 1682, but building did not stop there, the south porch being added as lately as 1969. The spire is 53m (174ft) high and had to be rebuilt in 1883 when the top section collapsed after being struck by lightning. That was not the only damage to have been sustained during its history: in 1646 there was a Civil War skirmish near the town resulting in fifty deaths and the church being damaged by cannonballs, the marks of which may still be seen on the east and west walls. There was also a fire causing damage to much of the interior.

The only monument of note in the church is in St. Peter's Chapel. Unusually this houses a tomb which has been used three times: by Viscount Lisle who died in 1356, in 1540 by Sir William Kingston (whose tomb was vandalized after the Civil War skirmish, presumably by townsfolk seeking vengeance), and then in 1623 by the Seaman family. The brass matrix is that of Kingston and his wife, the alabaster kneeling effigies being of Dr John Seaman and his wife.

The most interesting feature of the church is in the churchyard, with the finest collection of table tombs in the Cotswolds. Many tombs are the work of the Bryan family, local masons; the tomb of John Bryan (died 1787), a plain pyramid, is a complete contrast, a miniature of the Caius Cestius tomb in Rome.

Painswick Church and a table tomb.
(Below) Village Stocks, Painswick.

With their carvings of skulls and scrolls, the table tombs are fascinating, so good that a 'Tomb Trail' leaflet has been published, highlighting the best of the features. The tombs stand among Painswick's famous clipped yews. Local legends have it that either the yews cannot be counted or that there are ninety-nine, and any attempt to increase the number to a hundred fails, the new tree dying. In reality there are more than this number.

Each year in September the Clipping Ceremony takes place at the church, the Painswick children circling the building and joining hands. Despite the name, the ceremony has nothing to do with the yews, the name being derived from the Saxon word for circling.

The entrance to the churchyard from the main street is through a fine lych gate, built in 1901 but of old timbers from the belfry. Go through the churchyard and leave through the gate into Hale Lane. To the right from here, about 20m along the street, is a set of leg irons – the old village stocks. To the

right as you exit the churchyard is the Court House, a superb early seventeenth-century mansion built for a local cloth merchant. Walk ahead along Hale Lane, passing several fine old houses. Continue along St. Mary's Street, then turn left up Bisley Street. To the right, now, are some of the town's finest buildings. Byfield Home is Tudor, while the Chur is fourteenth century and was once a coffee house. Beside it is Little Fleece. It and Wickstone, next door, are also fourteenth century and once formed the Fleece Inn. The arch above Wickstone's ground-floor window once gave access to the inn's courtyard. At the crossroads turn left. To the left is Painswick Woodcrafts where Dennis French, a member of the Guild of Craftsmen, shows his work. Continue along New Street, passing the fine fifteenth-century, timber-framed Post Office on the right. Further on, opposite the church, is the Falcon Hotel, built in the early eighteenth century for the lords of the manor, the Jerninghams, whose family crest included a falcon.

About 800m from the centre of Painswick – take the B4073 towards Gloucester from the traffic lights – is Painswick House and its Rococo Gardens, the only complete garden of the period in Britain. The rococo period in garden design was brief, representing a transitional phase between the formal gardens (Italian-style) of the seventeenth century and the natural (English-style) of the next. The garden at Painswick House had been lost, but a painting of it in its prime (by Thomas Robins, painted in 1748), has allowed it to be recreated. The six-acre site is now a delight, with both formal areas (enhanced by curious structures, too small to be called follies), and natural landscapes.

Painswick stands close to the Cotswold Edge, which should be visited for the tremendous views it offers over the Severn Valley. One of the best is from **Haresfield Beacon**, which lies on the Cotswold Way. Head towards Stroud along the A46, turning right along the A4173 through **Pitchcombe** – where Pitchcombe House, a beautiful eighteenth- century mansion is worth noting – and Edge. Turn left to follow Scottsquar Hill. Ignore the road bearing left for Whiteshill and Randwick, old cloth-working

The Rococo Gardens, Painswick.

villages, but now village suburbs of Stroud, and bear right to reach a parking place at the top of the steep hill descending into Haresfield. Follow the Cotswold Way south to Haresfield Beacon where there is a promontory hillfort, the neck of the promontory defended by a ditch and rampart, the steep scarp slope providing the other defences. The ditch was dug in the Iron Age, but the site was so obviously excellent that the Romans also used it, as evidenced by a horde of Roman coins found there. From the Beacon the Severn's huge meander at Arlingham can be seen, as can the Welsh hills beyond. To the south the Cotswold Edge is clearly defined. A very fine short walk now follows the Cotswold Way eastwards to where it passes through the beautiful Standish Wood, or northwards to reach a stone that commemorates the raising of the siege of Gloucester on 5 September 1643.

Heading north from Painswick, along the A46, a left turn is soon reached leading to Painswick Beacon and the local golf course. The view westwards from here is as good as from Haresfield Beacon, but that along the Cotswold Edge is more restricted. On again, a road is reached, to the right, for Cranham. Our tour will take that road, but first two detours – one by road, the other by foot along a woodland path – are worthwhile.

The first continues along the A46, dropping down to Cotswold Edge to reach Prinknash Abbey on the left. The Abbey's name is pronounced 'Prinage' and not as spelled. The original house here was built in the fourteenth century as a hunting lodge and grange for the Abbot of Gloucester. At the dissolution the grange was sold, becoming a private residence: Prince Rupert used it as his headquarters during the siege of Gloucester in 1643. In 1888 it was bought by Thomas Dyer-Edwards. On his conversion to Roman Catholicism in 1924 he invited the Benedictine monks of Caldy Island to set up a community on his estate. The monks took over the house, following a bequest by the Earl of Rothes who had married Dyer-Edwards's daughter. In 1939 the monks began the construction of the new Abbey, though it was not completed until 1972. Despite its appearance – it looks much like the 'reconstituted' Cotswold stone that is now used for much building within the AONB – it is actually of Cotswold stone, from a quarry near the Guitings. The square-sided building is not to everyone's taste (the Abbey has been compared to a cinema), but is certainly distinctive.

The Abbey church may be visited, a worthwhile visit for the beautiful stained-glass, but most visitors come to see the pottery and the bird park. In the former the monks create a range of work with distinctive patterns and lustre that have become world famous. Other craft articles are also available.

The bird park, which is not managed by the Abbey, consists of nine acres of parkland with several lakes through which a range of wildfowl roam. The geese include snow and red-breasted from the Arctic, and Chinese bar-headed geese. There are also black swans and peacocks. In addition to the free-flying species there are aviaries for rarer breeds. There is also a deer park with fallow and muntjac deer.

Fallow deer at Prinknash Bird Park.

The walking detour follows the Cotswold Way through Buckholt Wood to **Cooper's Hill**. Buckholt Wood, together with Cranham and Witcombe Woods, form a large expanse of deciduous woodland (chiefly beech) alive with birds and animals. The Cotswold Way follows a delightful path through the wood to reach the top of Cooper's Hill down which cheeses are chased in one of the Cotswolds' most spectacular (and dangerous) festivals on the Spring Bank Holiday. The slope is 1-in-1 and 185m (200yd) long. From the top it seems difficult to climb down, and the prospect of

Spring morning, Cranham Woods.

109

hurtling down it in pursuit of a 3kg (7lb) cheese seems madness. It is easy to see why a cheese is rarely caught, and why injuries, including broken limbs and concussions, are frequent.

The origins of cheese rolling is not well understood, but similarities between the Cooper's Hill event and others elsewhere suggest that originally it was a flaming wheel that was rolled down the hill, usually at midsummer. This implies that the event has pagan origins, related to the imploring of the sun to return as the days grew shorter. Today's event at Cooper's Hill is a much shortened version of the one that was held in the last century, when the cheese rolling was just one aspect of a programme that involved races, dancing, bobbing for oranges or apples, wrestling and gurning (the pulling of faces through a horse collar – an event still practised in the Lake District). One surviving nineteenth-century programme also offered 'a bladder of snuff to be chatred for by hold wimming' – a prize of snuff for the old woman who talked (chattered) longest or loudest.

From the A46 follow the road through the woods towards Birdlip, ignoring the road on the right for **Cranham**, a pretty village nestling at the woodland edge. The Old House is a beautiful seventeenth-century Cotswold house with typical gables and mullioned windows, and the church has sheep-shears carved on the tower in honour of the wool trade.

The road reaches a junction with the B4070: turn left towards Birdlip, reaching the village at a junction. To the right is the village, but first turn left, descending steeply to reach the villages of Great and Little Witcombe, tucked below the Cotswold Edge. Close to **Great Witcombe**, which has a lovely little church with several survivals from an original Norman building, are the excavated remains of a Roman villa. Though not the equal of Chedworth, the site is an interesting one. The villa was probably built in the first century AD and was constructed on three sides of an open courtyard, with a small mosaic pavement and a fine bathhouse. The best of the excavated items are housed in the small site museum. The remains are now in the care of English Heritage.

The Romans would doubtless have approved of the planting of a vineyard at nearby **Little Witcombe**. At the Crickley Windward Vineyard visitors may wander through the vineyard and taste and buy the wines made from the six varieties of grapes grown.

Birdlip, set right on the Cotswold Edge, has a pleasant little church with a bellcote. The village is famous for the finds excavated from a nearby series of Iron Age burials which included the finest collection of jewellery from that period so far discovered in Britain. The most important item was the Birdlip mirror, one of only two so far discovered. The mirror, made in about 50BC, is a flat bronze disc about 15cm (6in) in diameter with an 8cm (3in) handle. It was made by the lost wax method and is engraved and inlaid with enamel. It may be seen in Gloucester Museum.

From Birdlip a short detour can be made to **Brimpsfield**, a manor given to Walter Gifford by William the Conqueror. The Giffords built a castle, but a descendant, John Gifford, rebelled against Edward II and was hanged for treason. The castle was demolished, though the line of the moat and walls can be made out in a field close to the church. The church will interest amateur (and professional) architects: how is the tower held aloft?

From Birdlip our route follows the B4070 towards the A417, but turns left just before reaching the main road, to reach a car park at **Barrow Wake**, on the very edge of the Cotswold scarp slope. The view from here is magnificent, taking in Crickley Hill to the right, Witcombe Woods to the left, the Witcombe villages at the base of the slope and, beyond, Gloucester, the tower of its cathedral easily visible.

Crickley Hill is our next objective: turn left along the A417 to the roundabout by the Air Balloon Inn. Go straight across, following the B4070 to Cheltenham (not the A436 towards Stow and Oxford), soon turning left into the hill's Country Park. The hillfort that tops Crickley Hill has been extensively excavated; information boards give details of the Neolithic and Iron Age fortresses. The details of the gateway of the last Iron Age fort,

Leckhampton Hill, looking towards Cheltenham.

designed so that attackers were turned to offer their unshielded right sides to the defenders (most people, then as now, being right-handed) are fascinating. From the Country Park the Cotswold Way can be followed north-eastwards into Short Wood, a lovely little beech wood.

The Cotswold Way is also the best means of exploring nearby **Leckhampton Hill** (to the right as you follow the B4070 towards Cheltenham). The scarp slope here was quarried earlier this century, but the venture was not a success, with accidents

The Devil's Chimney, Leckhampton Hill.

from the very start. At the opening ceremony in October 1922 the then Minister of Labour cut the first turf with a specially-made silver spade that bent beyond repair on impact with the ground. The stone was transported down incredibly steep inclines, the ropes hauling the wagons sometimes breaking, sending wagons ladened with stone hurtling downhill to cause havoc at the bottom. As if that were not enough, the explosives used caused the stone (which here is very fragile) to crack, and so annoyed the nearby house owners that the company was taken to court and ordered to stop. Stop it did, for ever, exactly three years to the day from the spade's bending. The quarrying did, however, produce one famous Cotswold landmark, the Devil's Chimney. This is believed to have been created by the quarrymen just for the fun of doing it. Today it is held in place by liberal quantities of concrete and is out of bounds to would-be climbers.

Follow the B4070 past the edge of Leckhampton Hill (the Devil's Chimney is just visible from the road in winter when the trees are bare), passing through Leckhampton village to reach Cheltenham College's Thirlestaine Hall.

ADDRESSES AND OPENING TIMES

MISERDEN PARK GARDENS,
Miserden *(01285 821303)*
❖
OPEN: April–Sept, Tues–Thurs, 9.30am–4.30pm

PAINSWICK WOODCRAFTS (Dennis French),
New Street, Painswick *(01452 814195/01453 883054)*
❖
OPEN: Jan and Feb, Tues–Sat, 9.30am–4.00pm
(closed for two weeks in Jan);
March–Dec, Tues–Sat, 9.30am–5.00pm
(also Bank Holiday Mon and Mon in Aug, 10.00am–5.00pm,
Sun from May–Sept, 2.00–5.00pm)

PAINSWICK ROCOCO GARDEN,
Painswick House *(01452 813204)*

❖

OPEN: second Wed in Jan–Nov, Wed–Sun,
11.00am–5.00pm (also Bank Holiday Mon and daily in July
and Aug, same times)

PRINKNASH ABBEY,
near Painswick *(01452 812239)*

❖

OPEN: Abbey Church: all year, daily, 5.00am–9.00pm;
see notice at church for services
POTTERY: tours (lasting 20 min) available all year,
Mon–Sat, 10.30am–12.30pm, 1.30–4.00pm
POTTERY SHOP: all year, daily, 9.00am–5.30pm

PRINKNASH BIRD PARK,
near Painswick *(01452 812727)*

❖

OPEN: all year, daily, 10.00am–5.00pm; closed Christmas
Day, Boxing Day, New Year's Day and Good Friday

GREAT WITCOMBE ROMAN VILLA
(01452 425674/0117 975 0700)

❖

OPEN: exterior is open at any reasonable time; guided tours
are available on specific dates; telephone for details

CRICKLEY WINDWARD VINEYARD,
Little Witcombe *(01452 863555)*

❖

OPEN: Easter–Christmas, Tues–Sat, 12.00–5.30pm;
Christmas–Easter ring beforehand

(Opposite) The yew cross at Wyck Rissington Church

Stow and the Oxfordshire Cotswolds

Stow-on-the-Wold

'Stow-on-the-Wold,
Where the wind blows cold.'

The couplet may not be great poetry, but it does offer an accurate view of Stow's position, exposed on the high wolds. At 230m (750ft) above sea level, Stow is the highest Cotswold town. In fact, the well-known couplet had a final line – 'And the cooks can't roast their dinners', recalling an ancient saying of the townsfolk that of the Greeks' four elements, Stow had no earth, no water and no fire, but plenty of air.

In early Saxon times a Christian hermit called Edward is said to have lived by a well on the site of what is now the town. Edward's hermitage became famous as a 'stowe' or holy place, the name being transferred to the town that grew up around it. It is an attractive story, and doubtless has its roots in truth, but the town's position on Fosse Way and at the intersection of other northern Cotswold tracks meant that it was always a favoured site. Today eight roads converge on the town, though because of modern bypass systems none of them actually runs through The Square, the town's market place. It was in The Square that the greatest of Cotswold sheep fairs was held annually. During his tour of the area in 1724 Daniel Defoe visited it and was amazed to see no fewer than 20,000 sheep awaiting sale. The Square's buildings form an irregular area, its shape designed to give maximum shelter to animals and merchants. Into The Square ran narrow alleys called 'tures' through which sheep were herded from outlying pens. The Market Cross, at the southern end of The Square, was apparently erected to remind farmers and merchants alike of the need for civilized, honest behaviour. The Cross's headstone was added only in 1995: its side panels depict the Crucifixion, St. Edward the Confessor, the Civil War and the wool trade.

A tour of Stow should start from the Cross, heading northwards along the left-hand side of The Square. Most of the shops to the left have interesting facades, but that of St. Edward's

House, with its fluted Corinthian pilasters, is the most picturesque. It dates from the early eighteenth century and is
named, as is much else in the town, after the hermit, though it
is debatable whether he was actually ever a saint. A little further
along is the appropriately-named Crooked House, dating from
the mid-fifteenth century. It is assumed that subsidence has
caused the tilt. To the right, in the centre of the southern part of
The Square, is St. Edward's Hall, built in 1878 with money from
unclaimed deposits in the town's Savings Bank. The Hall was
erected as a public meeting hall and now houses the library. The
spire was for a bell to summon the fire brigade.

On The Green, at The Square's northern end, are the old
town stocks, the holes set so far apart that discomfort must have
been added to ritual humiliation for those sentenced to be held
there. Now walk down The Square's eastern side, passing several excellent seventeenth-century buildings to reach the King's

Stow-on-the-Wold.

St. Edward's House, Stow-on-the-Wold.

The Keyt Memorial, Stow Church.

Arms, an old coaching inn. A town legend has it that Edward IV considered the inn the best on the coach road from London to Worcester, though there is no evidence for an inn there until the end of the Civil War. Charles I is reputed to have stayed there before the Battle of Naseby.

Continue along the edge of The Square and then Digbeth Street to reach the Royalist Hotel, parts of which date from the tenth century and which claims to be Britain's oldest inn. As well as being an inn (at one time called the Eagle and Child) the Royalist has also been a hospice and a chapel.

Turn right along Sheep Street, taking a 'ture' on the right to return to The Square. Now turn left to visit St. Edward's Church. The original building here was Norman, though little of that remains, there having been alterations and additions over a period of several hundred years. On 21 March 1646 the final battle of the Civil War was fought near Stow, forces of about 3,000 men facing each other. The Royalists under Sir Jacob Astley were heavily defeated and Astley, together with some 1,500 other Royalist prisoners were confined to the church, with the wounded being laid out in Digbeth Street. It is said that the street ran with blood. There is only one memorial to a victim of the battle, to Hastings Keyt, a Royalist commander. On the memorial, an incised slate in the floor of the chancel, Keyt is shown in the Royalist 'uniform' of a lace-edged sash, with helmet, pike and gauntlets in two corners and skulls in the other two. In 1992 the Sealed Knot society placed a memorial in the churchyard to all who fell in the battle. After serving as a prison, the church was declared ruinous but was restored in 1680.

Inside, it is the stained glass and the rood beam, added as a memorial to those who died in this century's wars, which take the eye. The two clerestory windows are pre-Raphaelite, the rest being Victorian mass-produced, but of a very high standard. The boldly coloured west window is particularly good. Finally, as you leave, look for the painting of the Crucifixion to the right of the door. It is attributed to Gaspar de Crayer, a contemporary of Van Dyck and Rubens.

To the east of Stow are two attractive villages. **Oddington** is a strung out village with Upper and Lower ends. In the church (tucked away along a lane running south from the lower village), a superb fourteenth-century wall painting was discovered in 1913 under a whitewash coat believed to have been added by, or before, the Puritans. The painting displays the Last Judgement in graphic detail. Further on, **Adlestrop** has two fine houses. Adlestrop House is seventeenth century, but altered, and was once the Rectory. When Theophilus Leigh was the vicar here, his niece Jane Austen occasionally came to stay. Adlestrop Park was a grange of Evesham Abbey, passing to the Leigh family at the dissolution. The gardens were laid out by Humphrey Repton. The nameplate from the now-closed railway station is preserved in the village as a reminder of the poem by Edward Thomas.

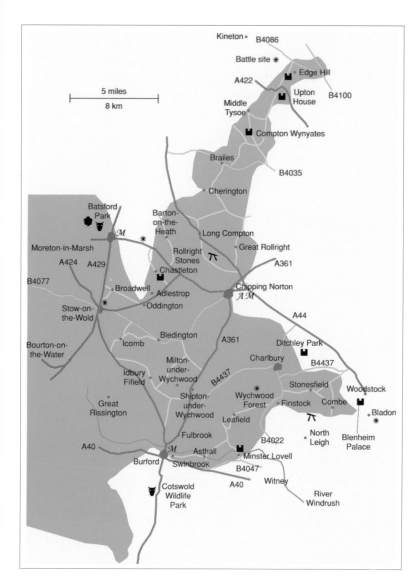

Kineton •   B4086

Battle site ✳

A422   Edge Hill   B4100

Upton House

5 miles
8 km

Middle Tysoe •

Compton Wynyates

Braíles

B4035

• Cherington

Batsford Park

Barton-on-the-Heath

Long Compton

Moreton-in-Marsh   Rollright Stones   • Great Rollright

A424   A429   Chastleton   A361

B4077   Broadwell   Adlestrop   Chipping Norton

Stow-on-the-Wold   • Oddington   A44

Bourton-on-the-Water   Bledington   A361   Ditchley Park

Icomb   Milton-under-Wychwood   Charlbury   B4437

Idbury
Fifield   B4437   Stonesfield   Woodstock

Shipton-under-Wychwood   Wychwood Forest   Finstock   Combe   • Bladon

Great Rissington   Leafield   North Leigh   Blenheim Palace

Fulbrook   B4022

A40   Asthall   Minster Lovell

Burford   Swinbrook   B4047   Witney

A40   River Windrush

Cotswold Wildlife Park

TOUR 5: Stow and the Oxfordshire Cotswold

At its north-eastern corner the Cotswold AONB extends into Oxfordshire as far as Woodstock and northwards as far as Edge Hill. Purists may complain, but there is no doubting the interest that lies in these far-flung areas.

Leave Stow northwards, along the A429 to Moreton-in-Marsh, soon reaching a road to **Broadwell** on the right. The village is centred on a large green and is notable for an alabaster effigy in the church showing Herbert Weston, who died in 1633, and his wife kneeling at a prayer desk.

Moreton-in-Marsh confuses most first-time visitors by being so-named rather than 'in-the-Marsh', which is what they would expect. It is unlikely that there has ever been a marsh hereabouts, the name deriving from the town's position on the *march*, or boundary of several ancient regions. These eventually became counties, the Four-Shires Stone, just a little way to the east, marking the spot where Gloucestershire, Worcestershire, Warwickshire and Oxfordshire met. Today only three counties meet there, Worcestershire having been pushed westwards.

Moreton is an airy place, the wide main street successfully absorbing the main A429 as it bisects the town. It was once an important market town and, standing on a crossroads, a coach stop, several old coaching inns surviving in the High Street. In one, the White Hart, Charles I is reputed to have slept on 2 July 1644, the date 1782 inscribed on the building presumably (if the story is true) dating its rebuilding. In 1826 Moreton was a terminus for an ambitious venture when a horse-drawn tramway was opened to Stratford-upon-Avon, 25km (16 miles) to the north. The tramway was made redundant by steam power, but the new railway also came to Moreton making it one of the few Cotswold towns to have been served by it. The town doubled in size within a few years of the railway's arrival.

In the centre of the High Street stands the Redesdale Market Hall, built in 1887 by Baron Redesdale, the lord of the manor,

Redesdale Market Hall, Moreton-in-Marsh.

as the plaque on the south wall notes. It is an excellent building with a steeply-pitched roof and a delightful clock turret. Across the road from the Hall is the Curfew Tower, one of few now surviving in Britain. Fire curfews date from Norman times, bells being rung to warn villagers to cover their fires, fire being one of the greatest hazards of medieval Britain. The tower here dates from 1633 and was rung at 5am and 8pm in summer, and 6am and 8pm in winter until 1860. This relatively recent date followed a bequest of Sir Robert Fry who became lost on his way home one foggy night and followed the ringing bell to the town. He left money for the bell to be rung (and for the clock to be wound), but by 1860 the townsfolk had had enough and the curfew ceased. Interestingly, Moreton is now the home of the Fire Service Training College. The base of the tower is the old town lock-up.

Close to the High Street, in Broadway Road the Wellington Aviation Museum and Art Gallery has memorabilia of Wellingtons and other aircraft, together with sculptures, prints and paintings. A shop sells aviation books and videos.

From Moreton head east along the A44 towards Chipping Norton and Oxford, passing the Four-Shires Stone to reach a turning to Chastleton, on the right. Chastleton is a small village dominated by Chastleton House, a Jacobean manor built on land owned by Robert Catesby, one of the Gunpowder Plotters. The house was altered at later times, but has retained much of its original character, including the marvellous Long Gallery with its plaster ceiling. There is also some beautiful panelling. Legend has it that the owner at the time of the Civil War fled here from the Battle of Worcester and hid in a secret room behind the panelling when Parliamentarian soldiers arrived to search for him. The soldiers decided to stay the night – in the same room as the man was hiding, and he was able to escape only when his wife drugged the soldiers with laudanum. The house is now owned by the National Trust. At the time of writing it is closed for restoration but it is hoped it will be reopened in 1998.

Turn left for **Barton-on-the-Heath**, once the home of Robert Dover, the reviver of the Olympick Games on Dover's Hill near Chipping Campden. The village has an attractive green with an old well at its centre, and a church that is believed to stand on the site of an Anglo-Danish church, the most southerly such site to have been so far identified. From the village take the road eastwards to reach the A3400 at **Long Compton**. The village is rather spoilt by the main road, but has some lovely houses and a fine church. The church is reached through a delightful two-storeyed, thatched lych gate (believed to have once been a house from which the lower storey has been removed). The upper storey is now the church's store room.

Long Compton church and lych gate.

North of Long Compton the AONB pushes a finger north-wards to Edge Hill. To visit the scarp overlooking the battlefield, follow the minor road to **Whichford**, passing excellent woodland on the right. Whichford also has a village green, and a beautiful early eighteenth-century Rectory. Turn left to Stourton, a small hamlet that is now virtually connected to larger **Cherington**, to the west. Here there is a fine Manor House and a church housing a rare canopied chest tomb from the fourteenth century, on which lies an unknown man who is not (hence the rarity) in knight's armour. Turn right through Sutton-under-Brailes to reach the larger village of **Brailes**, a village divided into Upper (to the left) and Lower (to the right) sections. The church, in the lower village, has an elegant Perpendicular tower.

Castle Inn, Edge Hill.

Go through Lower Brailes, then left to reach Winderton. Bear right through the village, then left at a junction to pass **Compton Wynyates**. Many claim the view of this early Tudor house to be the most perfect in England, the beautiful house set off by fields and woodland and with a little church tucked away to one side. Building began in 1480, but took forty years to com-plete. The house was begun by Edmund Compton, whose son William was a young page to Prince Henry, later Henry VIII, and was knighted by him on the battlefield of Tournai where William showed great courage. Later, after he had become King, Henry stayed at the house. Compton Pike, opposite the House, is a spire marking the spot where a beacon was lit after the defeat of the Spanish Armada. On the hill above the house stands a superb windmill which may be reached by footpath. The view across Warwickshire from the mill is superb.

Follow the road past Compton Wynyates, soon bearing right along a road to Tysoe, a village divided into three, rather than two, parts. Go through the village to reach the A422 and turn right to climb the steep Sun Rising Hill. Turn left to reach Edge Hill. The battle fought at the foot of the steep hill on 23 October 1642 was the first real battle of the Civil War and was as indecisive as it was bloody. Charles I was marching on London from Worcester, but decided to turn and fight the Parliamentarian army of the Earl of Essex rather than allow it to harass the rear of his army. Consequently he lined his 13,000 infantry and cavalry along the foot of the hill and waited for Essex's 12,000 men to advance from Kineton. The battle started with artillery bombardments from both sides, followed by a Royalist cavalry charge. The Royalist cavalry was eventually stopped by Parliamentarian reinforcements arriving from Warwick, among whom was a young captain, Oliver Cromwell.

After the cavalry charge King Charles ordered his infantry forward. As he prepared to lead them, the infantry commander, Sir Jacob Astley, said his famous prayer: 'Oh Lord, Thou knowest how busy I shall be this day. If I forget thee, do not Thou forget me.'

After the battle, in which an estimated 5,000 men were killed, both sides claimed a victory neither deserved, though the King's position was slightly the better, giving him a superiority he was not to maintain.

The battlefield lies outside the AONB, though that is of little consequence as no access to the site is permitted; there is a monument beside the B4086 towards Kineton. A good view of the field can be obtained from the Castle Inn with its embattled tower. It is often said that King Charles watched the battle from this tower, but as it was not built until over a hundred years later that can be dismissed. The tower is also claimed to be a monument to the battle, but even that is not clear. It was built by Sanderson Miller, the squire of Rodway, and may just have been a folly tower.

From Edge Hill return to the main road and turn left, soon reaching the entrance to **Upton House** on the right. The House is reached by a long drive between lawns and fine trees. It was built, in sumptuous style, in 1695 and stands in front of terraced gardens and parkland with ornamental lakes. But despite the attractions of the architecture and the grounds, it is the art collection which draws visitors. The collections include Sèvres porcelain, Brussels tapestries, Chelsea figures, eighteenth-century furniture and paintings by Holbein, Canaletto, El Greco, Hogarth and Constable. The House and its collections were given to the National Trust by the second Viscount Bearsted.

From Upton House return to Long Compton and head south-east along the A3400, towards Chipping Norton. Soon, a turn on the right leads to the **Rollright Stones**. There are actually three groups of stones, a circle known as the King's Men, a single standing stone (the King) and a group of five stones known as the Whispering Knights. The name refers to an old legend (first written down by the Elizabethan traveller Camden in 1586), that the stones result from a meeting between a king, his army and a local witch. The king told the witch that he intended to conquer the whole of England, and the witch, exasperated by his arrogance, set him a rhyming puzzle. She told him to taken seven long steps, as long as he could, and, from where he finished, 'if Long Compton thou can see, King of England thou shall be.' Knowing the local geography the king scoffed and marched forward, only to find his view blocked by a low mound of earth. The witch promptly turned him and his army to stone. The whispering knights were a small group of men who had moved away from the main army to plot the king's overthrow. Other local legends suggest that the stones of the circle cannot be counted – if you count more than once you will obtain different answers – and that the stones descend to a spring to drink when Long Compton church strikes midnight on 31 December.

In practice the stone circle is simply that – a late Neolithic or Bronze Age circle, probably erected 3,500 to 4,000 years ago. The single standing stone probably formed part of the same ritual site, while the knights are the remains of a burial chamber: four upright stones and a capstone.

The village of **Great Rollright**, for which the stones are named, lies on a flat hill top, exposed to winter's winds. The church, the village's most interesting feature, has a tympanum with a fish among geometrical designs.

From the stones or the village, return to the main road and head towards Chipping Norton, turning right at the round-about to enter the town. **Chipping Norton** is a market town with few concessions to tourism, though its inns are popular with passing trade, just as they have been since the days of the mail coaches to London. The White Hart Hotel in Market Place was a coaching inn, the Blue Boar, at the northern end of Middle Row which leads off the Market Place, catering chiefly for market traders. Across from the Blue Boar is the town's old Guild Hall, now home to the Tourist Information Office. Nearby are the town's theatre (housed in what was once a Salvation Army citadel) and the craft shop of the Oxfordshire Craft Guild,

Market Square, Chipping Norton.

where visitors will find pottery, jewellery, and wood and glass work. Along Church Street, almost opposite the theatre, are the Cornish almshouses, built in the mid-seventeenth century by Henry Cornish. The observant will notice that although there are eight houses (built originally for poor widows; after modernization there are now only four houses) symmetry demanded there were nine chimneys.

Beyond the almshouses is St. Mary's Church, another wool church, though despite Chipping Norton's wealth, not the equal of the great wool churches to the west. Inside there are some good brasses, but the main item of interest is the delicate fifteenth-century font. To the north of the church, on private land, are the earthworks that are all that now remain of the town's Norman castle.

Return to the Market Place (where markets are still held on Wednesdays) and cross to High Street, dominated by the massive, though elegant, Victorian Town Hall which stands on the site of the old market hall. Across from the Hall is the Town Museum with items and photographs that explore the history of the town from prehistoric to modern times. Chipping Norton was the birthplace of Warren Hastings, the first Governor-General of India, and also of William Smith, who produced the first geological map of England. On the other side of the Town Hall from the museum is New Street, the A44 for Evesham. Following this road for a short distance allows a view of the Bliss Tweed Mill, another Victorian building, with an extraordinary chimney emerging from a dome-topped round tower. The owners of the luxury flats into which the mill has been converted doubtless feel differently about the place than the townsfolk who once worked within its somewhat forbidding walls.

From Chipping Norton, take the A361 south towards Shipton-under-Wychwood, soon turning left along a minor road to **Chadlington**, set above the Evenlode Valley. The church here has an interesting collection of gargoyles on the outside, and an equally good collection of carved corbels on the inside. To the north of the village (head north from the hamlet of Dean and follow a path across Little Hill) is the Hawk Stone, a 2.25m (8ft) standing stone probably dating from the Bronze Age.

From the village, follow the signed road for Charlbury, turning right along the B4026 to reach the town. The name **Charlbury** is Saxon, meaning 'Ceol's fortified place', presumably a clearing in the huge Wychwood Forest. Certainly the market town we see today started as a village after a section of the Royal Forest had been cleared. As a contrast to the wool towns to the west, Charlbury's prosperity, particularly in the eighteenth century, was based on glove-making. The Napoleonic Wars put a temporary end to the trade, but it soon reviewed and was an important local industry until this century. The town is attractive, but, as at Chipping Norton, has made few concessions to tourism. The best of the old houses are in Thames Street, where Armada Cottage and Old Talbot are late sixteenth century. The church, close to the river, is mainly seventeenth century, with a fifteenth-century tower. If the tower is open, it is worth climbing for the view across the river to Cornbury Park and the Wychwood Forest. On the other side of the river is the railway station, designed by Isambard Kingdom Brunel.

The House in Cornbury Park was the home of the Earl of Leicester, the favourite of Elizabeth I. It was here, legend has it, that he was visited by the ghost of his wife who told him that he had only ten days to live. Despite the help of doctors and a trip to Bath for the waters, the prophecy came true: the Earl died on the tenth day. There were those who saw vengeance in the tale, the Earl's wife Amy Robsart having been found dead in very mysterious circumstances with a broken neck some years before; her death paved the way for a potential marriage between the Earl and Elizabeth I.

Today the Park is owned by Lord Rotherwick. Its central 650 acres form a National Nature Reserve where fallow deer, amongst other wildlife, roam. Surrounding the Reserve are a further 650 acres of SSSI (Site of Special Scientific Interest). As the Park borders the Wychwood Forest, the entire area makes up one of southern England's most significant wildlife habitats. The Park is circled by a fine walk from its North Lodge (reached by following Church Street, turning left along Park Street and then right along a line that crosses the railway and the river) via Finstock.

To the north of Charlbury and outside the AONB, is **Ditchley Park**, built in the early eighteenth century for the Lee family, one of whose descendants was Robert E. Lee, the Confederate General in the American Civil War. The House was used by Winston Churchill and allied commanders in the Second World War during the preparations for D-Day. It is now an Anglo-American Conference Centre, and is occasionally open to the public.

From Charlbury take the B4022 towards Witney, soon bearing left to reach **Stonesfield**, a large village whose name evokes memories of famous local quarries. Continue to Combe, which has a neat village green overlooked by a fine old inn. The church has a flagstone floor and a stone pulpit built into a wall, an unusual feature. There is also a fine fifteenth-century font and a medieval wall painting of the Last Judgement. Close to the village – follow the road to the station and go under the railway – is Combe Mill, a nineteenth-century sawmill with a working beam engine. There is also a Cornish boiler and two other original steam engines, together with some old farming equipment and a working forge.

Take the road to the sawmill, continuing through Long Hanborough to reach the A4095. Turn left to reach Woodstock and Blenheim Palace, passing through Bladon along the way.

Woodstock is a fine old town, though much of its eighteenth-century elegance has been blighted by unsympathetic modern building. The town has an enviable history: Henry I had a deer park and one of the world's first zoos here; Henry II kept 'Fair Rosamund' at Woodstock Manor and visited her frequently; the Black Prince was born here in 1331; and Princess Elizabeth was imprisoned here by her half-sister Queen Mary. The Manor House that saw this parade of royalty was almost

Woodstock.

destroyed during the Civil War, though Vanbrugh lived in what remained when he was working on Blenheim Palace.

Being a royal demesne made the town prosperous, a prosperity its market enhanced, as did the glove-making industry which was already well established by the time Queen Elizabeth I returned to the scene of her imprisonment. Within the town there are still some fine old houses: the Bear Inn is probably the oldest, parts dating from the thirteenth century, though it was rebuilt in the sixteenth. The Town Hall was built in 1766 by the then Duke of Marlborough. The parish church, to the south by the main road, has Norman origins, but has been considerably altered. The tower is eighteenth century, while inside there is a fine fourteenth-century octagonal font. But pleasant though Woodstock undoubtedly is, to most visitors it is merely a stepping stone to **Blenheim Palace**, one of the greatest houses in Britain.

Sarah Jennings was the favourite companion of Queen Anne before she came to the throne in 1702, and it was due mainly to Sarah that her husband John Churchill was made the first

Duke of Marlborough. But Churchill was an extraordinary man in his own right, Britain's greatest general since Henry V, and one of the great commanders of all time, being both a brilliant organizer and a brilliant strategist. As commander of the British army he was largely responsible for curbing the expansionist ambitions of Louis XIV of France. The telling blow was the defeat he inflicted on the French army at Blenheim on 13 August 1704 as co-leader of a British–Austrian force.

In gratitude for the victory, which not only restricted the French but made Britain one of the foremost European nations

Blenheim Palace.

at a time when it had become little more than an off-shore island, Anne gave the Duke the Royal Manor of Woodstock. Parliament also granted £500,000 (a vast sum for the time) for the building of a house, to be called Blenheim Palace in honour of the great victory. Sir Christopher Wren, the greatest architect of the day was the natural choice to design the house, but Sarah, Lady Marlborough, rejected his plans in favour of a design by Sir John Vanbrugh. The foundation stone was laid in 1705.

Vanbrugh's plan was for one of the most lavish houses in Britain, so sumptuous in scale and detail that Parliament's cash

was inadequate, the Duke having to find another £50,000 to complete the project. The house, in warm stone, covers three acres, large enough to ensure that it remains elegant despite its detail, yet intricate enough not to look bulky. The rooms and contents of the Palace need a guide book to themselves. The Great Hall is over 20m (67ft) high and the library, with its 10,000 volumes, almost 60m (187ft) long. There are paint-ings by Reynolds and Van Dyck, wood carv-ings by Grinling Gib-bons and a spectacular ceiling painting of the Battle of Blenheim by

133

Sir James Thornhill, completed in 1716. There is also an exhibition dedicated to the life of Sir Winston Churchill, with a considerable number of his personal items. Sir Winston was born at Blenheim on 30 November 1874. The room in which he was born is the centrepiece of the exhibition: its simplicity, with a plain brass bed and equally plain furnishings, is a marked contrast to some of the Palace's grander rooms.

To complement the Palace, the parkland around it (over 810ha, 2,000 acres) was landscaped by Henry Wise, Queen Anne's own gardener, though Wise's design was considerably modified by Capability Brown to whom much of the credit for the park's natural look must go. Brown dammed the River Glyne to create a huge lake, crossed by Vanbrugh's Grand Bridge. The lake is now home to flocks of waterfowl and visitors can take a trip along it in a launch or borrow a rowing boat for their own tour. From the Palace there is a view along the Grand Bridge to the Column of Victory on which stands a statue of the first Duke in the toga of a Roman emperor. Close to the Orangery (which was used by the Duke as a picture gallery, but later as a theatre) is the formal Italian Garden. Away from the Palace are the Pleasure Gardens in which are the world's largest symbolic hedge maze, a herb and lavender garden, a butterfly house, children's adventure play area and an amusement area with a putting green, giant chess set and inflatable castle. There is also a cafeteria.

After Churchill's death in January 1965 there was a state funeral followed by a burial, at his own request, in the churchyard at **Bladon**. The church is an unassuming Victorian building, the chief interest being in the churchyard. Churchill lies beneath

The Tomb of Winston Churchill, Bladon.

a slab inscribed simply with his name and dates, close to the graves of his father Lord Randolph Churchill and his mother Jenny Jerome, the daughter of an American newspaper magnate.

After visiting Bladon, follow the A4095 towards Witney. Go through Long Hanborough, then turn right along a minor road for Finstock, and right again towards Stonesfield to reach the **North Leigh Roman Villa**. This large villa was built around a courtyard. Its best preserved section is a mosaic floor with a geometric pattern in reds and browns. The style of the mosaic leads experts to believe that it was made by workers from Corinium (Cirencester). The villa is in the care of English Heritage and may be viewed at any time, the mosaic being protected by glass. The villa is reached by a long track (about 600m, 660yd) from the road.

Continue along the road from the villa, ignoring a road to the right for Stonesfield, to reach **Finstock**, a pleasant little village described by John Wesley as being full of 'plain and artless people', which seems a backhanded compliment, if one were intended at all. Wesley did also point out the 'delightful solitude' of the village, so perhaps he did like it. He was correct about the solitude; Finstock's closeness to the wonderful Wychwood Forest, and the apparently timelessness of the local country giving it an air of tranquillity. From the village head west, crossing the B4022 and skirting the edge of Wychwood Forest, an ancient Royal Forest – a hunting ground reserved for royalty and their guests – to reach **Leafield**. Here the medieval cross on the green was restored by the villagers in 1873 in thanks for 'deliverance from the scourge of smallpox'. The church, with its lovely pyramidal spire, is Victorian. Turn right in Leafield to reach Minster Lovell.

Minster Lovell is claimed by many to be the loveliest village in the Windrush Valley. The river is crossed by a fifteenth-century bridge, the Old Swan Inn being of the same age. For the rest, there is no one building that stands out, the whole being a delight. Close to the northern bank of the Windrush and at the edge of the village are the ruins of Minster Lovell Hall, one of

The ruins of Minster Lovell Hall.

the AONB's most romantic sites. The Hall was built in the fifteenth century by the Lovell family and is the setting for two very similar legends. The first concerns Francis, Earl Lovell, a real man. He is said to have fled Bosworth battlefield and gone into hiding (having been implicated in many of Richard III's schemes), only to reappear as a supporter of Lambert Simnel who, it was claimed, was one of the 'Princes in the Tower'. When Simnel was exposed as a fraud, Lovell retreated to the Hall where he lived in a secret room which could be opened only from the outside. His hiding place was known only to his manservant, but the man died suddenly, leaving Lovell entombed. Interestingly, in 1708 during repairs to the Hall a secret chamber was indeed found and contained the skeleton of a man, seated at a table, and that of a dog.

The second story is known as the Mistletoe Bough legend and concerns a young girl (perhaps newly-wedded) who, during a friendly game of hide-and-seek, hid in a large chest. The lid closed on her and, unable to escape or make enough noise to be heard, she died of starvation, just as Francis Lovell had. Her body was found only years later by accident.

Though the Hall is in ruins, the medieval circular dovecote has been restored. The site is in the care of English Heritage and may be visited at any time. The nearby church, dedicated to St. Kenelm of Winchcombe, houses an effigy of William Lovell who built the hall and rebuilt the church.

From Minster Lovell follow the B4047 towards Burford, then turn right to **Asthall**, a perfect little village beside the Windrush. Here, in true English village style, an Elizabethan Manor House stands beside a delightful church, the pair overlooking a collection of little cottages. In the church there is an interesting fourteenth-century effigy of Lady Joan Cornwall in a wimple.

Follow the Windrush westwards, soon reaching a right turn to **Swinbrook**. In the church here there are two triple memorials to members of the Fettiplace family. The six, all male, lie in effigy on their right sides staring out at the visitor, 'like passengers on an old steamboat' as someone once remarked. In the churchyard are the graves of the Mitford sisters Unity and Nancy who spent their childhoods in the village.

To reach Burford do not turn right to Swinbrook (or return across the river after your visit) and continue beside the River Windrush.

Asthall.

Burford is often called the most beautiful town in the Cotswolds and, if the distinction between a village and a town is made, it certainly has a good claim. Its steep High Street, heading north towards the triple-arched bridge over the Windrush, is lined with attractive and historically interesting buildings, and the church with its tower and elegant spire is equally good. When the Romans came to the Cotswolds they crossed the Windrush at nearby

The River Windrush at Burford.

Asthall, perhaps seeing the steep valley side near Burford as too gloomy for a settlement. The Saxons chose the town site, naming it for their fortress beside the ford. The medieval packhorse bridge which replaced the ford (or perhaps an earlier bridge) is still in service today, its restricted width requiring single line traffic (and traffic lights).

Burford was the first Cotswold town to receive a market charter, its later prosperity being based on the market and the wool merchants who lived in the town. To explore it start at the top of High Street and take a gentle downhill stroll. The return up the hill will be rather more energetic. On the upper part of High Street, known simply (and accurately) as The Hill, there are old houses on both sides, perhaps dating from the late fifteenth century; but the first major interest is the Tolsey, on the left. Here the town's Guild of Merchants met and tolls were collected from market traders. The exact date of the twin-gabled building is not known: it was certainly built before the mid-sixteenth century and is probably late fifteenth century. The pillared frontage was to allow market stalls to be erected out of the rain, and stalls are still placed there today. The Tolsey is used by Burford Town Council and also houses a museum of local history, with early charters, maces and seals.

The Tolsey stands at the corner of Sheep Street which has several fine early houses. The Bay Tree Hotel dates from the mid-seventeenth century, while the Lamb Inn, in part fifteenth century, claims to be the oldest inn in town. The Tourist Information Office occupies the town's old brewery. Back in the High Street, opposite Witney Street (on the right), is the arch of the former George Hotel. The legend is that Charles II and Nell Gwynne spent a night here. To the right now there are some excellent early houses and the old Methodist Chapel (now a private home). John Wesley was active in west Oxfordshire, visiting Burford several times.

On the corner of Priory Lane (to the left) is Falkland Hall, built in the late sixteenth century by one of the town's richest clothiers. Priory Lane is named for a small sixteenth-century daughter house of Keynsham in Somerset. It is now a private residence. Turn right along Church Lane, passing the magnificent sixteenth-century school to the left. Ahead are the town's almshouses, founded by Richard, Earl of Warwick, in 1457. It is said that it was here that Warwick promised to make the Earl of March King (he became Edward IV) so earning his nickname 'Kingmaker'. Bear left to reach the church.

Burford Church is almost as large as some cathedrals, a tribute to the wealth of the town's merchants who enlarged it progressively from its beginnings as a small Norman building until the decline of the wool trade, though the major fabric of the church was completed by 1475 when the tower and spire were added. Inside there are several excellent monuments. The finest is that to Sir Lawrence Tanfield and his wife, which almost entirely fills the north transept chancel. Sir Lawrence was Lord Chief Baron of James I's Court of Exchequer, a grand title, in keeping with the grand way in which he ran his life. His wife was even worse, riding roughshod over the locals and effectively annexing the chapel for her husband's tomb without the courtesy of first asking permission. The tomb is a remarkable work for all that, the pair lying in effigy as though in a four-poster bed, with their only daughter at their head and their only grandson at their feet. As an aside, a local legend claims that if the water in the River Windrush fell so that the bridge's third arch were dry, the Tanfields would return to Burford, and superstitious locals could be seen bucketing water into the river whenever there was a drought – just in case.

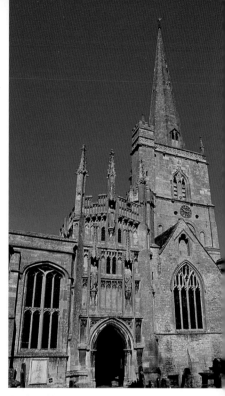

Burford Church.

Below the nave arch, look for the beautiful brass to John Spicer, who died in 1437, and his wife Alice. The couple face each other, kneeling and in period costume. Another fascinating memorial is that to Edmund Harman, barber to Henry VIII, on the wall of the north aisle. At the base of the memorial are the relief carvings of Harman's sixteen children, only two of whom outlived him and his wife Agnes. However, interest centres on two other aspects of the memorial. The first relates to the figures at the four corners of the epitaph. They are almost certainly carved from drawings in a Flemish book of 1540 which showed Amazonian Indians. As such they are the first representation of New World Indians in Britain; but why are they on Harman's tomb? The other interesting fact is that, despite the epitaph, Harman and Agnes do not lie below the tablet. They lived for seven years after it was erected and are buried in nearby Taynton. And by the time of his death Edmund had clearly forgotten the note about 'his only and most faithful wife Agnes' and had remarried.

Finally, make your way to the font. It is not often that a church is proud of graffiti scratched on its stonework, but that on the font 'Anthony Sedley, 1649, Prisner' is part of Britain's history. On 1 May 1649, just three months after the execution of Charles I, over 1,000 troops of Cromwell's New Model Army refused to obey an order to go to Ireland. A few days later they left their camp, heading westwards and reaching Burford on 13 May. There, despite assurances from Cromwell and Fairfax, they were attacked. One man was killed and many escaped, but about 340 were herded into the church. Anthony Sedley was one of these. On the morning of 17 May the prisoners were taken on to the church roof to watch as a token group of three of them (nominally the ringleaders) were shot. The rest were released with a reprimand. Today it is usually said that the mutineers were 'Levellers' but it seems highly unlikely that they were. There was a group of reformers in the army who had drawn up an 'Agreement of the People', demanding more social justices (and given the name Levellers at the time because it was – wrongly – said they believed that incomes and property should be 'levelled' – equalized), but the mutineers' grievances were more to do with their having not been paid for several months and not wishing to go to Ireland.

A Woolsack Tomb in Burford churchyard.

From the churchyard, with its superb collection of 'woolsack tombs', the representation of a woolsack on the table tombs being an indication of the debt owed to the wool trade by the entombed, go along Lawrence Lane to return to the High Street. To the right is a fine group of sixteenth-century weavers' cottages. Turn left to climb back to the start of the tour.

To the south of Burford, and just outside the AONB, the **Cotswold Wildlife Park** has a collection of animals, in large enclosures, in the 65ha (160 acres) of parkland around a fine Victorian Manor House.

From Burford cross the Windrush and bear right along the A361 to **Fulbrook**, where the Dunsdon brothers lived. They were notorious local criminals and the probable origin of 'Tom, Dick and Harry' as an expression for everyman. Dick is believed to have bled to death after his brothers deliberately cut off his arm when he had been handcuffed during an attempted arrest; Tom and Harry died on Gloucester's gallows. The story is told that Tom had been badly hurt in one leg during their arrest and was limping painfully. As they made their way to the scaffold Harry encouraged his brother, telling him that it made little difference that he had only one good leg as he had so little time left to stand. The brothers' bodies were gibbeted locally (to encourage others) on a tree still marked as Gibbet Tree on maps (on the right-hand side of the A361 to the north of Capps Lodge Farm).

Continue along the A361 to **Shipton-under-Wychwood**, a large, picturesque village with a large green. On one side of it is the church, an almost pure early English building with a lovely spire. Inside there is a good fifteenth-century stone pulpit. On the other side of the green is the Shaven Crown Hotel. This magnificent building was once the hospice of Bruern Abbey, to the west. The hotel lounge was the Great Hall and one of the rooms was once the hospice chapel. This ancient use explains the hotel's name, which is unique in Britain. The hotel sign, of a head with a monkish tonsure, is delightful. At the southern end of the village is Shipton Court, a beautiful early seventeenth-century building, notorious in its day

Shipton-under-Wychwood.

because of the violent death of the butler of Sir John Reade, the owner, in the mid-nineteenth century. Reade was a drunkard, his butler often joining him for prolonged drinking bouts. One night the butler fell and was impaled on a firedog. Reade claimed that the fall had been an accident, but the villagers talked darkly of murder during a brawl. Whatever the truth, accidental death was the verdict, though Reade became a sober man immediately afterwards and died full of guilt and remorse. His ghost is said still to haunt the Court despite several attempts at exorcism.

From Shipton, a short detour eastwards reaches **Ascott-under-Wychwood**, another attractive village with some lovely old houses and a Norman church with a tower that has an unusual, semi-detached look.

From Shipton, turn left to reach **Milton-under-Wychwood**, with a church by G. E. Street, whom we have already met in Toddington. To the north of the village is Bruern Abbey, though nothing remains of the original Cistercian house. After the dissolution the abbey was dismantled, the present house dating from the eighteenth century. From Milton take the road to **Fifield**, where the church has an interesting brass to Mary Palmer, complete with her eight children. Despite the humorous possibilities behind the name of village's inn – the Merrymouth – it is actually named for the Norman Lord de Muremuth. Continue to **Idbury**, a tiny village where Sir Benjamin Parker, the designer of the Forth Railway Bridge lies buried.

From Idbury there are alternative routes back to Stow. One heads northwards to **Bledington** and the B4450, turning left along it. Bledington has a church with superb fifteenth-century stonework and stained glass, the result of the village having once been owned by wealthy Winchcombe Abbey. Manor Farm is believed to be on the site of a rest-house for Winchcombe monks.

The alternative route heads westwards through the tiny Westcote hamlets to reach the A424. Turn right towards Stow, soon passing a turn, to the right, for **Icomb**. In the church here is a stone effigy of Sir John Becket, who died in 1431 and was the builder of lovely Icomb Place.

ADDRESSES AND OPENING TIMES

WELLINGTON AVIATION MUSEUM AND ART GALLERY,
Broadway Road, Moreton-in-Marsh
(01608 650323)

❖

OPEN: all year, daily except Mon, 10.0am–12.00pm and
2.00–5.30pm

CHASTLETON HOUSE (National Trust),
Chastleton, near Moreton-in-Marsh
(01494 528051)

❖

OPEN: currently closed for restoration;
telephone for details of reopening

UPTON HOUSE (National Trust),
near Edge Hill *(01285 670266)*

❖

OPEN: April–Oct, Sat–Wed, 2.00–6.00pm

MUSEUM OF LOCAL HISTORY,
High Street, Chipping Norton *(01608 658518)*

❖

OPEN: Good Friday–Oct, Tues–Sun, 2.00–4.00pm;
Bank Holiday Mon, same times

OXFORDSHIRE CRAFT GUILD SHOP,
7 Goddards Lane, Chipping Norton *(01608 641525)*

❖

OPEN: all year, Tues–Sat, 10.00am–5.00pm;

COMBE SAW MILL,
near Combe

❖

OPEN: some Sundays, 10.00am–5.00pm;
ask at Tourist Offices or telephone 01993 891785 for details

BLENHEIM PALACE,
Woodstock *(01993 811325)*

❖

OPEN: mid March–Oct, daily, 10.30am–5.30pm
(last admission 4.45pm)

TOLSEY MUSEUM,
126 High Street, Burford

❖

OPEN: Easter–Oct, Mon–Fri, 2.00–5.00pm;
Sat and Sun, 11.00am–5.00pm;
telephone *01993 823558* (Burford Tourist Office)

COTSWOLD WILDLIFE PARK,
Burford *(01993 823006)*

❖

OPEN: all year, daily, 10.00am–5.00pm;
4.00pm closing Oct–March;
closed Christmas Day

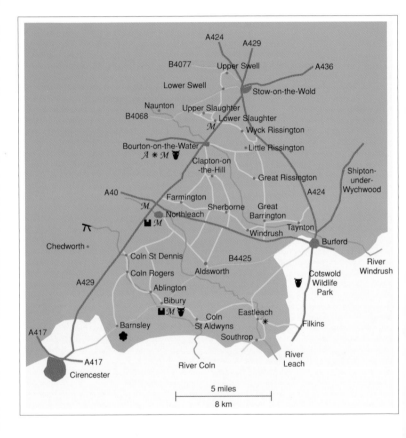

TOUR 6: Stow and the Cotswold Heartland

This short tour from Stow-on-the-Wold visits a number of villages acknowledged as being among the finest in the Cotswolds, as well as Bourton-on-the-Water, one of the area's most famous villages, and Northleach with its magnificent wool church.

From Stow, take the B4077 towards Broadway, soon reaching **Upper Swell**. There is little of this village, but what there is is wonderful: the bridge over the infant River Dikler; the weir and the old mill with its waterwheel; the little Manor House, standing on the site of a grange of Evesham Abbey; and the tiny church. There is a path on the western bank of the Dikler, the walk along it from Upper to **Lower Swell** being the perfect way to enjoy the two. Lower Swell is slightly larger and more airy and stands a little away from the river. It has several interesting architectural features. Spa Cottages, with their oriental features, were inspired by Sezincote, and Abbotswood (to the east beyond the river) was built in 1902 by Sir Edwin Lutyens. At one time it was the home of Harry Ferguson, owner of the tractor company. The original Norman church forms the south aisle of the present church, which is notable for its late nineteenth-century stained-glass and murals depicting the Passion.

From Lower Swell, ignore the B4068, taking the minor road heading south through lovely country to reach the Slaughter villages, justly famous for their picturesque qualities. The name derives from the Saxon for 'place of the sloes', not from any ancient bloody battle. We first go to **Upper Slaughter**. One rector of the much-restored church was the Revd F.E. Witts, whose *Diary of a Cotswold Parson* is one of the more entertaining books on the area. Witts, who died in 1854, was not only the village's vicar, but also the lord of the manor and lived in what is now the Lords of the Manor Hotel, a fine seventeenth-century building. The older Manor House is Elizabethan and is claimed by many to be the finest house of its period in the Cotswolds.

147

The Ford, Upper Slaughter.

At present the old manor is not open to the public. Close to the churchyard, the open square of cottages were remodelled by Lutyens. From them a road leads down to the River Eye, a tributary of the Windrush. Wander beside the river for charming views of the village and the surrounding country, and for a sight of the ford, which must still be negotiated by motorists and which is also crossed by the occasional herd of cows.

Lower Slaughter is a more formal village than its neighbour, not so pretty perhaps, but no less picturesque with its array of delightful cottages beside the Eye, which is crossed by little bridges. At one end of the village is a nineteenth-century mill, still with its waterwheel. The mill is brick built, but far from detracting from the stone-built cottages, its presence seems to enhance the picturesque qualities of the village. The mill is now a museum, with a small display of local crafts. At the other end of the village is the Manor House, built in the seventeenth century, and the village church.

From Lower Slaughter head east to reach the A429 and turn right, soon turning left to reach **Bourton-on-the-Water**. This is Broadway's only competitor as the tourist centre of the Cotswolds, an unashamed tourist trap, its every building seemingly dedicated to attracting visitors and relieving them of their cash. It is tempting to be cynical about Bourton and the extent to which it has become a tourist honeypot, but that would also be too easy. Peer beneath the tourist façade and what you find is a village that is genuinely pretty and worth all the time the visitor can spend in it, and, given the difficulties of attracting worthwhile jobs into an area such as the Cotswolds without destroying the very things which makes the area so appealing, what recourse is there except tourism? In days of increasing leisure and spending power, tourism is now, after all, an industry.

Lower Slaughter.

The known history of Bourton starts with the Iron Age settlement of Salmonsbury on the eastern side of the present town. This is an unusual site in being low-lying rather than on a hilltop, though it was protected by ditches and ramparts. The fort was occupied by the Romans, hardly surprisingly as Fosse Way runs just a few metres away. The Romans had a wooden bridge over the Windrush, but after their departure the Romano-British, and then the Saxons, reverted to fording the river. A stone bridge was built in the fifteenth century; the present bridge taking the A429 over the river dates from 1806.

It is believed that there was a Saxon church at Bourton from the early eighth century, and the Normans certainly had one. From Norman times Bourton's history was Cotswold history: the boom of the wool trade followed by a slow decline, arrested

Bourton-on-the-Water.

when tourists 'discovered' it. The centrepiece of the town is the river which is a foreground to all views of the main street. It is crossed at several places by pretty pedestrian bridges and populated by ducks which long ago learned that tourists mean food. A walk along the Windrush, crossing and recrossing it for a closer view of the wonderful stone cottages, needs no guide.

During such a walk the visitor will pass the Cotswold Perfumery (in Victoria Street on the southern side of the river – the opposite side from the High Street) which explores the history and nature of perfumes and has a garden where the flowers needed for perfume production are grown, a compounding room where perfumes are created and a shop where they may be bought; then the Pottery in Clapton Row, close to the Perfumery, where John and Judy Jelfs show their distinctive range of handmade and hand-decorated stone and earthenware, and terracotta; then the Motor Museum and Toy Collection, housed in an eighteenth-century watermill in

Cotswold Perfumery, Bourton-on-the-Water.

Sherborne Street, close to where it crosses the Windrush, which has around twenty cars and motorcycles from vintage models through to the 1950s and a toy collection covering the same period; next the model railway, in High Street, with OO/HO and N gauge railways carrying forty British and European trains, and a model and toy shop; after that the Village Life Exhibition in the Old Mill, with a reconstructed Edwardian village shop (complete with bedroom, bathroom and kitchen), an old blacksmith's forge and a collection of village memorabilia; and finally and perhaps best of all, the Model Village, behind the delightfully named Old New Inn on the High Street, with its stone-built model of Bourton itself on a 1:9 scale. The model includes, of course, a model of the model.

Birdland, in Rissington Road, at the south-eastern end of the town, has a number of aviaries and a tropical house, lakes with penguins, flamingos, swans and ducks, small parks with deer, South American rheas and storks, and a pets corner. The Dragonfly Maze, also in Rissington Road, was created by Kit Williams (author of *Masquerade* and designer of Cheltenham's Regent Arcade clock) and opened in 1997. The maze has 400m (440yd) of yew/trellis fencing and a fabulous central pavilion decorated with mirrors, tiles, sculptures and automata designs by Williams. Solving a riddle reveals a golden dragonfly.

From many places on a tour of Bourton the parish church, with a curious leaded dome sitting on top of its tower, can be seen. The first church was Norman, but of this only the rebuilt chancel remains, St. Lawrence's now being a fine example of nineteenth-century building. Inside there is some excellent carved wood, the painted reredos showing scenes in the life of Christ, and the oak screens showing the coats of arms of lords of the manor. The beautiful silver candlesticks are by D.T. Hart, the Chipping Campden silversmiths.

From Bourton, follow Sherborne Street southwards, climbing on to the wolds. At the high point of the road, a turn to the right leads to Farmington, but before going that way, continue ahead to reach **Clapton-on-the-Hill**, from where there is a fine view across the Windrush valley. The pleasant little village has a tiny church, claimed to be the smallest in the Cotswolds, with an indulgence carved on the northern spring of the chancel arch, a rare feature. The indulgence is carved in Latin and in translation reads, 'Whoever shall say three times devoutly a *Pater* and an *Ave* on his knees and in person, Lo! there is a reward then and there of a thousand days'. By comparison with normal medieval indulgences this is an astonishing offer.

Turn right and follow the minor road south to **Farmington**, a pleasant little village with a green on which there is an octagonal pumphouse with gables and a delightful cupola. From the village take the minor road to Northleach, avoiding the traffic on the A429.

Until 1984 **Northleach** suffered from having the main A40 running along the High Street, the traffic causing regular chaos and also adversely affecting the magnificent houses which line the street. The bypass has brought tranquillity, not only for the villagers but for visitors wishing to enjoy the village, and has prevented further damage to the buildings.

A tour of the village must start at the church. There was just a small hamlet beside the River Leach when in 1220 Gloucester Abbey, which owned the land, obtained a charter from Henry II for the holding of a weekly market. The first church was begun soon after, though virtually nothing of that survives. What we now see is the great fifteenth-century wool church (one of the three which, by common consent, are the best of the superb Cotswold wool churches, the other two being at Cirencester and Chipping Campden). The exterior of the church is magnificent, its soaring pinnacles and windows all pointing to heaven, but the real treasures are inside. The Northleach memorial brasses comprise the finest collection *in situ* in Britain, almost all of them to wool merchants, many of them with their feet on woolsacks. The earliest brass is from about 1400, to an unknown merchant and his wife (in the north aisle); the finest (though opinions differ) being that of 1458 to John Fortey, who was largely responsible for the rebuilding of the church. Fortey's is a huge brass, over 1.5m (5ft) long, lying beneath the north arcade. In it, Fortey is shown in a gown with collar and cuffs, fastened with a belt.

There is one particularly interesting item which appears in the memorial to John Taylour, his wife and fifteen children, in the south aisle. At the base of the brass is a woolsack, a sheep, a shepherd's crook and a pair of wool shears, a comprehensive list of the items that brought Taylour his wealth.

A detail from the Taylour Brass, Northleach Church.

From the church the visitor soon reaches the Market Place. To the right, is the beautiful Tudor House. Tradition has it that this was John Fortey's house. Opposite it is the Dolls House, the Cotswolds' only shop specializing, as the name suggests, in dolls' houses and dolls' house furniture, much of it craftsman-made. On the other side of High Street from the Market Place is a marvellous array of eighteenth- and nineteenth-century houses, some of them old coaching inns from the days when Northleach lay on the main coach road from Gloucester to London. Opposite the Dolls House is Keith Harding's World of Mechanical Music, a museum housed in the Oak House, a superb seventeenth-century house that was once an inn. The museum's collection is of self-playing instruments, from musical snuff boxes to large pianos. There are also automata and antique clocks. The collection is presented as entertainment as well as education and is enormous fun. There is also a shop where pieces may be bought. To the right (at the eastern end of the High Street, called, with formidable logic, 'East End') are the Dutton Almshouses built by Thomas Dutton, who stipulated that only women could occupy them.

From the Market Place a left turn is worthwhile, just to stroll along High Street, savouring the house façades. Almost opposite the Antelope (which was built before 1576, as in that year the town decided that it should be the only inn allowed at this end of the street) is a small cottage called The Guggle. The origin of the name is not understood, though it is believed that it is from the same root as Guiting (gushing) and so implies that there was a spring nearby. From the cottage an underground tunnel leads off. It has been romantically suggested that the tunnel lead to the church (though quite why is not explained), but it seems more likely to have been a quarry shaft.

From The Guggle it is possible to walk to the Cotswold Countryside Collection on the junction of the old A40 and the A429, but there is a large car park for those wishing to drive. The collection is housed in the remains of the Northleach House of Correction, built in 1791 as one of Gloucestershire's 'country prisons' – an enlightened idea of Sir George Onesiphorous Paul, a county magistrate. The prison housed a courtroom and a number of cells for local miscreants committing relatively minor offences. The courtroom and some cells form part of the museum. The collection is of old agricultural equipment, from wagons to basic tools. In the main building, as well as the courtroom and the cells there is a 'Below Stairs' exhibition with items from the Victorian kitchen and

The Countryside Collection, Northleach.

wash-house, and another on the history of local farming. There is also a temporary exhibition centre.

From the museum, follow the A429 southwards to Fossebridge where it crosses the River Coln. Now turn left, following the Coln through some of the most delightful of all Cotswold villages. The first is **Coln St. Dennis**, named for a Parisian church granted the manor in the wake of the Norman conquest. The church is early Norman, but with a fifteenth-century tower and, inside, a strange collection of grotesque heads as corbels. These too are original Norman work. From the village, narrow roads follow both bends of the river, that on the northern bank soon reaching Calcot, a pleasant little hamlet. **Coln Rogers**, the next village on the southern bank, has a largely Saxon church. One feature of this, the outer face of a round-headed window in the north wall which is cut from a single block of stone, is both distinctively Saxon and very rare. As at the earlier Coln village, the addition to the name dates from the period immediately after the conquest, in this case a knight who took the name Roger de Gloucester.

From Coln Rogers the single valley road crosses the river twice before reaching the hamlet of Winson and, beyond, the larger village of **Ablington**, a wonderfully picturesque place with two fine houses. Ablington Manor is late sixteenth century, while the later Ablington House is enhanced by two stone lions that once graced the Houses of Parliament. Beyond Ablington is **Bibury**, the undoubted highlight of the Coln Valley. William Morris claimed that Bibury was the most beautiful village in England. There is strong competition for the title, and many would contend that the way Bibury drifts along the main road through it, with no defined heart, counts against it. But in its favour are the wonderful buildings, particularly Arlington Row, which is as perfect a terrace of Cotswold stone cottages as exists, and the way the River Coln may be used as a foreground for most views.

Arlington Row stands on the site of a wool barn of the Bishop of Worcester. The cottages are seventeenth century and

Arlington Row, Bibury.

were occupied by weavers who would have used the mill leat (a diverted stream that fed Arlington Mill before returning to the Coln) for washing their cloth. The delightful aspect of the cottages is that they are not symmetrical, with odd gables and dormers and even changes of ridge line. Today the cottages are owned by the National Trust, though they are private homes and not open to the public. From the cottages a tiny bridge crosses to Rack Isle, between the leat and the river. Here cloth was 'racked' for drying. The island is now a wildfowl reserve.

At the other end of the island from the Row is Arlington Mill, reached along the main road – The Street – or by following Awkward Hill (!) and Hawkers Hill. Where Hawkers Hill reaches the main road, turn left to see the Catherine Wheel, a fifteenth-century inn, or right for the mill. Domesday Book records two mills at Bibury, but Arlington is known with certainty only from the early seventeenth century. At that time it was a cloth-fulling mill, though by the nineteenth century it had become one of the area's largest corn mills, with a steam engine to assist the waterwheel. The mill ceased operation in 1913. It is now a museum of its own milling machinery. There

Arlington Mill, Bibury.

is a museum shop and a licensed restaurant. Beside the mill is the Bibury Trout Farm where rainbow trout are bred for release into lakes and reservoirs throughout Britain. Visitors can also learn about fish breeding and may borrow rod and line to catch their own fish. Fresh and smoked trout can be bought at the farm shop.

From the mill head towards the Coln bridge. Beyond it is the Swan Hotel, built in the nineteenth century to replace an older inn, but extended in the 1930s. The hotel once housed the local court, the village lock-up being the octagonal, windowless building on the upstream side. Go past the hotel and walk along The Street, continuing past the Village Hall to reach St. Mary's Church. The church is Saxon, though this is only discernible on the inside as at a later time the church was extended around the Saxon shell. On the exterior north wall of the chancel there are the remains of an intricately carved Saxon cross shaft, while inside are the casts of two superb early eleventh-century Saxon gravestones. The originals are in the British Museum. The church also has some fine memorials, though the best tombs are those to rich wool merchants in the churchyard.

Behind the church is the Bibury Court Hotel, a fine building (part Tudor, but mostly seventeenth century) in a beautiful setting beside the Coln. Finally, from the church walk past the school and cross the main road to reach the Pigeon House, the oldest house in the village, dating from the fifteenth century. It is named for the nearby dovecote.

Before continuing along the Coln valley a short detour is worthwhile from Bibury, following the B4425 towards Cirencester to reach **Barnsley**. To the right as you enter the village is Barnsley Park, a Georgian baroque house standing in extensive parkland. Continue to the church, with its huge tiled roof and plain tower, beyond which is Barnsley House. The house dates from 1697 and was the rectory from the mid-eighteenth century until some sixty years ago. The house garden is open to visitors who will find rare shrubs, trees and herbaceous plants, a clever use of vegetables as decoration and two eighteenth-century summerhouses, one a Gothic alcove, the other a Doric temple. There is also a memorial to David Verey who created the garden.

From Bibury a fine walk follows the Coln to **Coln St. Aldwyns**, the village being viewed across the river as it is approached. It is another picture-book village with a green, a cluster of houses and an Elizabethan manor house. Parkland

Coln St. Aldwyns.

separates the village from **Hatherop** to the east and **Quenington** to the south. Hatherop Castle is nothing of the kind, being an Elizabethan manor house with an embattled tower. It is believed that William Burges (architect of Castell Coch in south Wales) worked on the house in the mid-nineteenth century when he was also assisting in the building of the church. Inside it there is a superb memorial to Barbara, Lady de Mauley, who died in 1844. She lies in marble effigy with free-standing angels at her head and feet. The parkland north of the village surrounds Williamstrip Park, a house built in the late seventeenth century for a Speaker of the House of Commons. Quenington Court stands on the site of a Preceptory of the Knights Hospitallers. The house is nineteenth century, but the dovecote, which retains its revolving ladder, is almost certainly fourteenth. The church has a very old (probably early twelfth century) tympanum above the north door with a representation of the Harrowing of Hell. God is represented as the sun's disk with a face.

From Hatherop or Quenington, head south-eastwards to **Southrop**, where John Keble, a leader of the Oxford Movement, was curate from 1823 to 1825. It was here that he wrote much of his best-known work *The Christian Year*. He also discovered the mid-twelfth-century font which had been built into the church doorway, presumably to protect it from the Puritans. The font, one of the greatest treasures of any Cotswold church, has relief carved panels beneath arches. One shows Moses with the Tables of Law; the others showing the Virtues

The font, Southrop Church.

trampling their respective Vices. The names of the Virtues are inscribed on the arches, those of the Vices are written backwards on the panels. Close to the church is Southrop Manor, a beautiful house dating, in its oldest parts, from the late

Keble Bridge, Eastleach.

Norman period. Beside the house is the River Leach, a lovely river which is now followed northwards, through the hamlet of Fyfield, to reach the twin Eastleach villages.

Eastleach Turville and **Eastleach Martin** are separated by the River Leach which is crossed by an old clapper bridge named for Keble who was rector at both churches for short periods. The closeness of the two churches is unusual, but arose from their having been granted to different lords of the manor after the Norman conquest. Turville, now the bigger village, was granted to a knight of that name, while Martin was granted to Richard Fitzpons who gave it to Malvern Priory. Later, both villages were given to Gloucester Abbey, the annual rent being a pound of beeswax. Today Eastleach Martin's church, the larger of the two, is redundant.

To the east of the Eastleach villages is **Filkins**. Though outside the AONB, few visitors will want to ignore the Cotswold Woollen Weavers, a working woollen mill where the production process can be seen. There is an exhibition on the wool trade and a shop where clothes and blankets may be bought. Also in Filkins are the Gallery and Studio where a number of artists and craftworkers complete and sell their work.

From Filkins take the A361 northwards to Burford, passing the Burford Wildlife Park. In Burford, cross the Windrush and bear left, soon turning left to follow the river to **Taynton**, once a quarrying village. Stone from here was used to build Blenheim Palace and several of the Oxford colleges. The village church has a tall, slender tower and, inside, some excellent carved corbels. Continue westwards to **Great Barrington**, a tidy village dominated by the huge Barrington Park on its western edge. The fine Palladian house here was built in 1736 for Earl Talbot and is beautifully positioned on a terrace overlooking the Windrush. The view of the river from the house did not meet with the approval of the Earl and Countess: to improve it a channel was dug so that a branch of the river would flow a little closer to the house. The landscaped parkland is dotted with summerhouses and folly buildings, and also has a domed dovecote, but is rarely open to the public. It may be glimpsed, as may the house, from the church which lies within the grounds. This should be visited for two excellent memorials. One, to Mary, the Earl's wife and the provider of

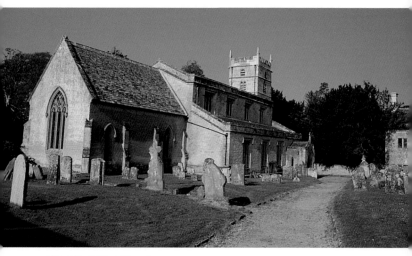

Great Barrington Church.

the cash for the house, is by Joseph Nollekens. In it, a bust of the countess is carried by a draped female figure. The other memorial is to two children of the Bray family who died of smallpox in 1720. It is in marble and shows the children being helped over the clouds to Heaven by a winged angel. This poignant, and beautiful, memorial is thought to be the work of Christopher Cass. The church also contains an effigy of Edmund Bray, an ancestor of the children, who died in 1620. He is shown with his sword on his left side: having killed a man during an angry exchange he was pardoned by Elizabeth I after remorsefully swearing that he would never again draw his sword with his right hand.

Across the Windrush lies **Little Barrington**, the road crossing Strong's Causeway. Thomas Strong, a Barrington man, is considered to have been the greatest stonemason of his time. Sir Christopher Wren thought so highly of him that he was the leading mason on St. Paul's Cathedral, laying the foundation stone. In his will Strong left money for a crossing of the Windrush to connect the two Barrington villages, stipulating that the bridge should be sufficiently wide 'that two men may go a front to carry a corpse in safety'. Thomas died before the completion of St. Paul's, but his brother, Edward, almost his equal in skill, continued the work and laid the cathedral's final stone. Little Barrington is grouped around a triangular green and has a strong claim to being the most delightful village in the Windrush valley.

Before heading north towards Stow, a short detour along the Windrush valley is worthwhile, heading westwards from Little Barrington to reach **Windrush**, named for the river. The church here has a famous south doorway, its arch having a double row of beakheads. There are some good memorials, one of the most interesting also being the newest, to a pilot who, in 1940, deliberately rammed a German bomber while on a flight from the local training strip in an unarmed plane.

Continue along the valley to **Sherborne**, a village strung out along the river and divided into two by Sherborne Park. The Park once belonged to Winchcombe Abbey. The area of to the south-west of the village is owned by the National Trust who have waymarked several nature trails through it. The house of the Park, also now owned by the National Trust but not open to the public, was built after the dissolution and modified by John Dutton who, though a Royalist officer, was also a friend of Oliver Cromwell. Dutton's memorial may be seen in the church. A nearby memorial to a later member of the family, James Lennox Dutton, is surely one of the most extraordinary such works in the Cotswolds. In it a life-sized angel, holding

The Dutton Memorial, Sherborne Church.

profiles of Dutton and his wife, tramples a skeleton representing Death, the upper part of the skeleton extended upwards in the best horror picture manner. The church also has a memorial plaque to James Bradley who succeeded Edmund Halley as Astronomer Royal. Bradley was born at Sherborne (we encountered him earlier as the colleague of Charles Mason of Sapperton).

From the far (western) end of the village the detour may be extended by heading south to the A40, passing a car park for the National Trust's Sherborne Park. Cross the A40 and go along the lane opposite, passing Lodge Park, to the right, a deer park established by John Dutton. Cromwell issued a warrant in 1655 allowing Dutton to take deer from Wychwood Forest to stock his park. The park lodge was built by Inigo Jones. At the T-junction beyond the park turn left to reach **Aldsworth**. The church here retains the original Norman building as its north aisle: look out for the superb series of gargoyles on the outer wall. In the churchyard are three grave slabs telling a poignant tale. In them lie a mother and two sons, both called Frederick. A local farmer and his wife, anxious for a son to inherit the land, were overjoyed when one was born after they had had two daughters. Sadly, at the age of eight young Frederick fell into a vat of home-brewed beer and was drowned. His mother was already pregnant again, and when she gave birth to a son he too was called Frederick. When he was seven this boy too died after a fall on to a pitchfork. The couple had no further sons.

Our tour continues from Great Barrington by heading north towards the Rissingtons. The first village reached – turn left off the northward road – is **Great Rissington**. The village lies on a steep hillside and has the distinction of having two greens.

Great Rissington.

164

At the base of the hill is the church in which, on the chancel nave arches, there are faint traces of medieval paintings. In the churchyard there are three slabs which are believed to have once marked the graves of crusaders. **Little Rissington** is also reached by a left turn from the northward road, opposite the now-disused airfield. It, too, has a hillside site, here looking out over the flooded gravel pits on Bourton-on-the-Water's eastern fringe. The pits are now home to numerous waterfowl. The church is set apart from the present village: medieval Little Rissington was closer to it, but was abandoned after the villagers were wiped out by the Black Death in 1347. In its churchyard lie a number of airmen who served at the nearby base.

Wyck Rissington is also reached by a left turn. It is the prettiest and also the most historically interesting of the three villages. It was here that seventeen-year old Gustav Holst played the hand-pumped organ in the church. He lived in the last cottage on the left along the lane linking the village with the A429. The churchyard has a rare Wellingtonia (an American tree, famously growing in the Sequoia National Park, called the Mammoth Pine or simply the 'Big Tree' in America, but named for the Duke of Wellington when it was first introduced to Britain) and a yew trimmed into a Living Cross. Inside the church there is a remarkable fourteenth-century stained-glass window depicting the Crucifixion. The cross is shown green (a rare coloration) and the moon (in the sun, moon and stars in the background) is red. It is believed that the pattern of sun, moon and stars, and the colour are a representation of the total eclipse of the sun in 1322. Also inside is a mosaic of the Wyck Rissington maze. In 1947 the vicar, Canon Harry Cheales, had a dream in which he saw people following the path of a maze. Realizing that mazes had long been seen as allegorical, representing man's tortuous path to heaven (Wolsey's maze at Hampton Court was constructed as an allegory), Canon Cheales believed the dream was a sign from heaven and began the construction of a maze to the pattern he had dreamt. He planted willow hedges along some 600m (660yd) of path, the

A mosaic of Canon Cheales Maze, Wyck Rissington Church.

maze being opened for the first time on Coronation Day in 1953. Sadly over the years the maze was neglected and, despite attempts to restore it, it was finally sold as a building site.

From Wyck Rissington follow the lane past Holst's cottages to reach the A429 and turn right to return to Stow.

ADDRESSES AND OPENING TIMES

Stow and the
Cotswold Heartland

THE OLD MILL,
Lower Slaughter *(01451 820052)*

❖

OPEN: all year, daily, 10.00am–6.00pm

Bourton-on-the-Water

BIRDLAND,
Rissington Road *(01451 820480)*

❖

OPEN: April–Oct, daily, 10.00am–6.00pm
(last admission 5.00pm);
Nov–March, daily, 10.00am–4.00pm
(last admission 3.00pm);
Bank Holidays apart from Christmas Day

COTSWOLDS MOTOR MUSEUM AND TOY COLLECTION,
Sherborne Street *(01451 821255)*
❖
OPEN: Feb–Nov, daily, 10.00am–6.00pm

COTSWOLD PERFUMERY,
Victoria Street *(01451 820698)*
❖
OPEN: all year, Mon–Sat, 9.30am–5.00pm;
Sun, 10.30am–5.00pm;
Bank Holidays apart from Christmas Day and Boxing Day

MODEL RAILWAY EXHIBITION,
High Street *(01451 820686)*
❖
OPEN: April–Sept, daily, 11.00am–5.30pm
(*SHOP:* Mon–Sat, 9.30am–5.30pm; Sun 11.00am–5.30pm);
Oct–Dec, Feb and March, Sat and Sun, 11.00am–5.00pm
(*SHOP:* Mon, Tues, Fri and Sat, 9.30am–5.00pm;
Sun, 11.00am–5.00pm)

MODEL VILLAGE,
High Street *(01451 820467)*
❖
OPEN: all year, daily, 10.00am–dusk; closed Christmas Day

BOURTON POTTERY,
Clapton Row *(01451 820173)*
❖
OPEN: all year, Mon–Sat, 10.00am–5.00pm;
Sun 10.30am–5.00pm

THE DRAGONFLY MAZE,
Rissington Road *(01451 822251)*
❖
OPEN: all year, daily, 10.00am–dusk

THE DOLLS HOUSE,
Market Place, Northleach *(01451 860431)*
❖
OPEN: all year, Thurs–Sat, 10.00am–5.00pm; some
Sundays, 11.00am–4.00pm; telephone beforehand

Cotswold Heartland

KEITH HARDING'S WORLD OF MECHANICAL MUSIC,
The Oak House, High Street, Northleach *(01451 860181)*

❖

OPEN: all year, daily, 10.00am–6.00pm (last tour 5.00pm);
closed Christmas Day

COTSWOLD COUNTRYSIDE COLLECTION,
Northleach *(01451 860715; 01285 655611 in winter)*

❖

OPEN: April–Oct, Mon–Sat, 10.00am–5.00pm;
Sun, 2.00–5.00pm

ARLINGTON MILL MUSEUM,
Bibury *(01285 740368)*

❖

OPEN: all year, daily, 10.00am–6.00pm; Oct–April, 5.00pm

BIBURY TROUT FARM
(01285 740215)

❖

OPEN: all year, Mon–Sat, 9.00am–6.00pm; Oct–April, 5.00pm;
Sun, 10.00am–6.00pm; Oct–April, 5.00pm

BARNSLEY HOUSE GARDENS,
Barnsley *(01285 740281)*

❖

OPEN: all year, Mon, Wed, Thurs and Sat, 10.00am–6.00pm

COTSWOLD WOOLLEN WEAVERS,
Filkins *(01367 860491)*

❖

OPEN: all year, Mon–Sat, 10.00am–6.00pm;
Sun 2.00–6.00pm; closed 25–31 Dec

FILKINS GALLERY AND STUDIO,
Cross Tree, Filkins *(01367 850385 (evenings))*

❖

OPEN: March–Oct, Mon–Sat, 10.30am–5.00pm;
Nov and Dec, Tues–Sat, 11.00am–4.00pm

(Opposite) Water pump, Castle Combe.

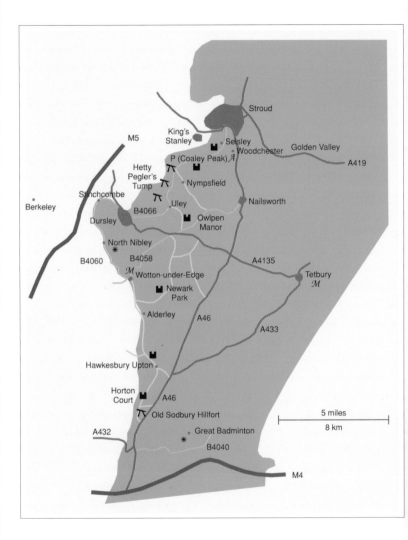

TOUR 7: Stroud and the Cotswold Edge

South of the A419, which links Stroud to Cirencester, are the Southwolds, geologically identical to the northern Cotswolds though the Cotswold Edge is lower and the dip slope a little less wooded. But the Edge is no less pronounced and the dip-slope countryside is equally attractive. There is, though, a distinct change of mood. At the eastern edge of the AONB there are still fine towns and villages – Tetbury, Easton Grey, Castle Combe – but the peacefulness and generally picturesque qualities of the northern area are replaced with busier towns and villages. The area, it seems, has maintained a better grip on time, changing with it rather than being timeless. Yet historically the interest remains high and, if there are fewer pretty places, they may still be found, along with many others that are attractive in different ways.

Stroud is a good example of the change in character of the AONB's town. It has an interesting history and fine buildings, yet is a bustling, modern, forward-looking place. It is also well placed to explore the Southwolds as far as the M4, though some may prefer the wold town of Tetbury.

Stroud was the centre of the wool trade for this middle area of the Cotswold and, later, the fast-flowing River Frome and its equally fast tributary streams powered mills that increased the prosperity when cloth was woven as well as the fleeces being sold. The area was especially popular with cloth-makers because it was believed that the water had peculiar properties which allowed a better 'fix' of red dyes. Whether this was true or not, much of Britain's red cloth was made here, including the scarlet tunics of the British army. It is an irony that, when the failure of the trade led to appalling local poverty and eventually to hunger riots, it was soldiers in Stroud-red tunics who were set against the rioters. The leader of the soldiers was James Wolfe, later to achieve fame but to lose his life at Quebec. Stroud's fascinating history may be explored at the town museum, which also includes a collection of early lawnmowers. The accepted inventor of the lawnmower, a Mr Pudding, was from the area. At the time of writing the museum is closed pending its probable resiting. It is scheduled to be re-opened during 1998, but visitors should enquire at the Tourist Information Office in the Subscription Rooms.

Stroud.

Stroud survived the crisis brought about by the decline of the wool trade better than some of the neighbouring towns and villages, the estimated 150 mills in the area reducing in number but maintaining enough capacity to ensure the town's survival. It was also able to take advantage of the Stroudwater Canal which linked it with the Severn and on to Midlands coalfields, importing cheap coal to run steam engines that were soon cheaper than water power. The canal, 13km (8 miles) long with twelve locks, was opened in 1779. It may still be seen to the west of the town.

The parish church, St. Lawrence's, is Victorian, apart from the fourteenth-century tower and is of interest chiefly for the tomb of John Hollings in the churchyard. This is in the form of a stepped pyramid topped by a rounded stone looking somewhat like a woolsack. It is said that the design of the tomb arises from a dispute between Hollings and another man who announced, before witnesses, that he hoped he lived long

172

enough to see Hollings safely underground. Gravely ill and realizing that he was to die first, Hollings arranged to be buried above ground in order to thwart his rival. The church-yard also holds the remains of Lt Joseph Delmont, claimed to be the last man in England to have died in a duel, in 1807. The duel was fought in the grounds of The Grange in Folly Lane.

Other striking buildings in the town include the Subscription Rooms, built in 1833 with a five-bay façade. The Rooms now house the Tourist Information Office and temporary exhibitions. Look, too, for the Town Hall, a late sixteenth-century building in The Shambles, named (as with its more famous namesake in York) from being the butcher's quarter of the old town.

From the centre of Stroud, head westwards along the A419 towards the M5, bearing left at the Cairncross round-about, then turn left along the B4066, head-ing uphill. The next right turn leads on to **Selsley** where All Saints' Church has stained-glass win-dows by William Morris and Pre-Raphaelite art-ists including Burne-Jones, Ford Madox Brown and Rossetti.

The William Morris Creation window, Selsley Church.

Many claim that the Creation window is the finest of Morris's stained-glass works.

The B4066 climbs across Selsley Common, then winds beside fine woodland to reach the **Coaley Peak** picnic site, on the right. Within the site are the remains of a long barrow (named for the nearby village of Nympsfield). As the earth mound and burial chamber capstones have been removed, the internal structure of the barrow may be seen. Excavations have revealed the remains of about twenty people. From the barrow a walk along the Cotswold Edge is worthwhile, reaching the panorama dial on **Frocester Hill** (though no climbing is involved to ascend it). The view from the hill is tremendous, taking in the whole of the Berkeley Vale, the River Severn and the Forest of Dean. On good flying

Nympsfield Long Barrow, Coaley Peak.

days there will also be hang-gliders, taking off from the hill itself, and gliders from the Bristol and Gloucestershire Club behind the scarp edge.

The village of **Nympsfield** is reached by turning left close to the Coaley Peak site. It is an attractive place with a pretty church and some fine buildings, of which the seventeenth-century Rose and Crown Inn is one of the best. From the turn off to the village, close to the B4066, a long track leads into Woodchester Park, a magnificent piece of country that is now an SSSI. Within the Park is **Woodchester Park Mansion**, claimed to be one of the great masterpieces of Victorian architecture despite its being unfinished. The house was commissioned by William Leigh and designed by Benjamin Bucknall, a friend of the French architect Viollet-le-Duc. Bucknall was a brilliant architect who spent much of his working life in Algeria. Work on the house was very slow and, after almost fourteen years, stopped altogether when the money ran out, but what was completed is remarkable. Everything in the house is of stone – including the drain pipes and the bath – and many of the details such as gargoyles and arches are of breathtaking quality. Equally interesting is that many of the materials used for

Woodchester Park Mansion.

construction – ladders, huge set squares and the wooden stone arch formers – may still be seen. Further along the B4066 from Coaley Peak there are two fine ancient sites. The first is **Hetty Pegler's Tump**, another long barrow, but here with its mound (42m long, 27m wide and 3m high – 140ft × 90ft × 10ft) intact. The barrow has a door – the key may be obtained from the next house along the road towards Uley – beyond which the low-stooping, torch-carrying visitor will find a long (7m; 22ft) passage with two pairs of side burial chambers. The barrow is named for Edith Pegler, the wife of Henry Pegler, who owned the field in which it stands in the seventeenth century, though quite why Hetty, as she was known, was chosen rather than some earlier owner is not known.

From the house where the key for the Tump is obtained, it is a short walk southwards to **Uleybury**, a huge Iron Age hillfort. The fort uses the steep scarp slope (which here forms a promontory), together with a ditch and rampart to enclose an area of 12ha (30 acres).

Continue along the B4066, now descending through trees to reach **Uley**, the village for which the hillfort is named. Uley was as famous as Stroud in the cloth industry, its speciality being a blue material of such a distinctive colour that it was known as Uley Blue. It was also famous for the militancy of its weavers, who formed themselves into a secret association, a forerunner of the trade unions. The seventeenth- and eigh-teenth-century merchants' and mill-owners' houses are found close to the village green, while the weavers' cottages lie further down the hill. From the top of the village a steep, narrow and unforgiving road drops down to reach **Owlpen Manor**, one of the most beautiful and romantically positioned houses in the Cotswolds. The house dates from the mid-fifteenth century, though it was enlarged in the eighteenth. It was abandoned in about 1850 and rediscovered by Norman Jewson (an architect who worked with Gimson and the Barnsleys at Daneway House). Jewson restored it and filled it with Arts and Crafts Movement furniture, this now being one of the highlights of a visit to the Manor. Others are the superb Great Hall and the Great Chamber with rare seventeenth-century painted cloth wall hangings. There are excellent terraced formal gardens, a restaurant in 'The Cyder House', and the old estate cottages have been converted into 'hotel' rooms.

From Uley, follow the B4066 downhill to reach **Dursley**. Posi-tioned between two Cotswold spurs, like pincers around the town, Dursley has few buildings from its wool trade days to add to the beauty of its setting, being now a modern town with local light industry to support the work opportunities that take its folk

Owlpen Manor.

into the Berkeley Vale and southwards to Bristol. As a wool town it prospered after Flemish cloth craftsmen had been enticed across the Channel by a promise of 'fat beef and mutton, good beds and better bed-fellows'. The bed-fellows would be the daughters of rich merchants who would want them to be married to the Flemish for their mutual profit. These daughters were 'of such beauty that the most envious foreigner could not but commend them'. The Flemish came in numbers (as the wold villages of Dunkirk and Petty – *petit* – France show), but whether the merchants were honest about their daughters was, presumably, a matter of opinion. Later, the same merchants became a byword for dishonesty, using several tricks to pass off short measure or poor quality cloth, to such an extent that 'you are a man of Dursley' was a significant term of abuse. When the wool trade finally died the town encouraged other industries. Listers, the marine diesel makers, were one of the more significant arrivals.

This gradual transition into a modern town meant the destruction of much of old Dursley. The Market Hall, at the centre of the town, was erected in 1738. The upper room was the old courthouse, the market being held in the arcaded lower area. Opposite the Hall is the town church, first recorded in 1221 when a murderer sought sanctuary within it. In the early fourteenth century the church was rebuilt around the old tower. Then, in 1480, a new tower and spire were added. By 1698 the spire was in poor shape and was patched up, at great expense, with several tons of lead and stone tiles. The work completed, a celebratory peal of bells was rung causing the spire to collapse. Fortunately it did not fall through the roof, landing outside the church: huge loss of life was therefore averted, but the falling spire did cause the end wall of the church to collapse killing several people. Queen Anne gave money for the rebuilding (explaining her statue in the Market Hall niche facing the church) but the funds would only run to a tower. The spire has never been rebuilt.

From Dursley follow the A4135 towards **Cam**, the town for which the nearby Cotswold outliers are named. Cam Long Down is the tent-shaped mass, while Cam Peak is the conical hill. These hills are already outliers of the scarp edge, but a good example of the initial phase of outlier production will soon be seen. Turn left along the B4060/B4066 for **Stinchcombe**, soon reaching a right turn for the village where there is a fine Manor House, built in 1837 and now an old people's home, and a church which, unusually, is dedicated to St. Cyr. Poised above the village is Stinchcombe Hill. The hill is almost triangular on its plateau top (on which there is a golf course), about 800m (875yd) wide along the base of the triangle, overlooking the village, and on each side, but only about 200m (220yd) wide at the triangle's point. In time the erosion processes which have caused this odd shape will gnaw through the plateau at the point, and the triangular mass will be partially detached from the main Cotswold mass. Once that occurs erosion will rapidly (on a geological timescale, that is) create a fully detached mass – just as at Cam Long Down and Cam Peak (and Downham Hill close to these two).

Continue along the B4060 to reach **North Nibley**. The most noticeable feature of the village actually stands above it, on Nibley Knoll. This is the Tyndale Monument, erected in 1866 as a memorial to William Tyndale, the translator of the Bible into English. Tyndale was born either at Nibley; or Cam; or perhaps at Slimbridge, there being evidence to support all three claims. For his heresy in translating the Bible Tyndale was executed by strangulation at Vilvorde in Holland, his body then being burnt at the stake. The monument can be climbed – see the plate on the door for information on obtaining the key – for a fine view over the Berkeley Vale and the Severn. Berkeley itself, with its castle (there is a nearby museum of Edward Jenner, the pioneer of inoculation) and a decommissioned nuclear power station, can be seen clearly.

At the far end of North Nibley from the monument is the church, a very neat building with a seventeenth-century tower. Inside, the memorial to Grace Smith, who died in 1609, includes a coloured, kneeling effigy. On the land below the church, Nibley Green, the last battle to have been fought in

Britain between private armies took place in 1470 between Thomas Talbot (the new Lord Lisle) and William, Lord Berkeley. The dispute was over the inheritance of the Berkeley estates after Thomas, Lord Berkeley (whose effigy is in Wotton-under-Edge church) died without an heir. There had been several lawsuits, but without a satisfactory outcome and finally Lisle, a hot-headed twenty-year-old, wrote to Berkeley challenging him to a duel. Berkeley's response was sarcastic, referring to Lisle's newly acquired title: 'Thomas Talbot, otherwise called Viscount Lisle, not long continued in that name, but a new found thing, brought out of strange countrys …' The furious Lisle gathered a thousand men and on 20 March 1470 arrived at Nibley Green. He charged Berkeley's men, of about the same number, immediately, but Berkeley was a shrewder general and had prepared his position well. Lisle's men were routed, about 150 being killed, including Lisle himself.

Continue along the B4060, which runs on a terrace of the Cotswold Edge, with the wooded scarp slope to the left and the Severn Vale to the right, to reach **Wotton-under-Edge**. On the corner of Long Street and Market Street stands Tolsey House, with its delightful dragon weathervane. The house is sixteenth century and was the old courthouse. It was also the site of the Pie Powder Court, named from the French *pied poudre* (dusty feet) which dealt with complaints against travelling market traders. In the old market area, called The Chipping, at the end of Market Street, there are some fine sixteenth-century half-timbered houses. The Heritage Centre in The Chipping explores Wotton's history. Further along Long Street, Berkeley House is an unspoilt Jacobean town house. Wotton's main treasures, though, are to be found close to the church. In Church Street are the Perry Almshouses, built in 1638 with money bequeathed by Hugh Perry, a local wool trader. The inner courtyard is wonderfully peaceful. The Falcon Hotel, beside the almshouses, is seventeenth century, while around the corner in The Cloud, the Ram Inn is much older, Wotton's oldest house. Its actual age is uncertain, but it is known that

The Perry Almshouses, Wotton-under-edge.

the builders of the church (completed in 1283) lodged here, so that it is at least 700 years old. It was originally timber-framed, but was later encased in stone.

The church, opposite the Ram, has a tower which many claim to be one of the finest in the county. Inside, the brasses of Thomas, Lord Berkeley and his wife Margaret, dating from 1392, are among the oldest in Britain and are also among the finest, being life-size and highly detailed. Thomas was a remarkable man, fighting against Owen Glendower in Wales and on several French campaigns. At the age of at least sixty he fought at Agincourt, dying of old age two years later. Thomas was fourteen when he married Margaret, who was then seven. Despite their ages, the marriage turned into a love match, Thomas never remarrying after Margaret's death at thirty.

From Wotton, take a minor road south to Wortley, where a left turn leads to **Ozleworth**, following the enchanting Ozleworth Bottom. Ozleworth Park is an eighteenth-century house: in the park stands a twelfth-century church with a rare hexagonal tower. Nearby, **Newark Park** is an Elizabethan hunting lodge (reputedly built with stones from nearby Kingswood Abbey after it had been dissolved) which was rebuilt by James

Wyatt in 1790. The house is now owned by the National Trust and is being carefully restored.

Back on the minor road, continue to **Alderley**, birthplace of Matthew Hale a seventeenth-century Lord Chief Justice who was deeply religious, a strong believer in witchcraft, and, as a judge, willing to condemn women to death for practising it. He is buried in the churchyard. Next to the church, Alderley House is a lovely Elizabethan building. There is a trout farm in the village where visitors may buy fish.

Continue southwards through Hillesley, a pleasant village, beyond which the road goes uphill towards Hawkesbury Upton, passing the **Somerset Monument**, to the left. The tower was erected in 1846 to the memory of General Lord Robert Somerset, a member of the Badminton Beaufort family, who fought at Waterloo.

At the monument – before reaching Hawkesbury Upton, a large village with an attractive pond – turn right, downhill, to **Hawkesbury** where there is a beautiful church with work from all the main architectural periods. Inside there is a finely carved fifteenth-century font. Bear left in the village, heading south towards **Horton** to reach beautiful Horton Court and church.

The Somerset Monument.

The Court consists of two distinct buildings. To the left as you approach is a Norman hall, all that remains of a twelfth-century house that was wholly domestic and completely unfortified, one of few from that period. The hall's roof is fourteenth century, but there have been few other changes. The hall houses a small museum of curios. The Court was added to the hall in 1520 by William Knight, the canon of the church. Knight was a lawyer and

181

one-time secretary to Henry VIII who acted for the King in Rome when he was attempting to divorce Catherine of Aragon. Knight's coat-of-arms, granted to him by Henry, are set above the door of the court. In the court's gardens there is a loggia (also built by Knight) with medallions of Roman emperors.

The church beside the Court is fourteenth century, but much modified. It is notable for the memorial to Anne Paston who died of 'a most tedious and painful sickness', a remarkably honest statement for a church epitaph.

Bear left at the T-junction in Horton village, following the narrow road to **Little Sodbury** where the church is dedicated to St. Adeline, the only such dedication in Britain. The church is Victorian, built on the site of one in which William Tyndale preached while he was tutor at the nearby manor house. The pulpit has panels depicting Tyndale the following Reformation martyrs: Cranmer, Hooper, Latimer and Ridley. Little Sodbury Manor was built in the fifteenth century and was once the home of Sir John Walsh who acted as King's Champion at Henry VIII's coronation. Henry and Anne Boleyn stayed at the manor many years later. Though altered and added to, it retains many original features. The Great Hall is among the

Horton Court.

finest of its type and is virtually unchanged. It was probably in the hall that William Tyndale made his oft-quoted remark to a visiting church dignitary that, if God spared his life, he would 'cause the boy that follows the plough to know more of the Bible than thou doest'. The sentiments behind the words led to Tyndale's translation of the Bible, but also contributed to the establishment fury which led to his death. Above and behind the manor, which is occasionally open to the public, is a well-preserved Iron Age hillfort.

From Little Sodbury follow the road beside the church to reach the A46 and turn left along it. Ignore the right fork for Tetbury, continuing northwards. The tree-topped mound on the right opposite the left turn to Kilcott is **Nan Tow's Tump**, a large Bronze Age round barrow named for a local witch who, according to legend, was buried upright (hence the mound's size) to prevent her return from the grave. From the A46, turn right for **Leighterton**, a plain village whose Norman church was virtually annihilated by Victorian restorers. Opposite the next right turn (also to Leighterton, the village being the target for a whole cluster of minor roads), a turn left follows a farm lane to Boxwell Farm, beyond which a walk reaches **Boxwell Court** and church. The fifteenth-century Court was the home of Matthew Huntley in 1651; Huntley brought Charles II here after the Battle of Worcester. The story goes that Huntley's wife, fearful of a search of the house, persuaded the King to sleep in the barn. Later, from his exile in France, the King sent Mrs Huntley a turquoise ring which is still in the family's possession. To the north of Boxwell, and reached by an equally unforgiving lane from the A46, is Lasborough Park, a fine seventeenth-century mansion. Neither of these two excellent houses is currently open to the public.

Just beyond the Lasborough turn, a road on the left leads to **Newington Bagpath**, a delightful hamlet with a church showing remains of a Norman building, and the well-defined motte of a Norman motte-and-bailey castle.

Follow the A46 to a crossroads with the A4135 and turn left for a short detour to **Kingscote**. In the church here, Catherine

Kingscote (of Kingscote Grange, a house that had been in the family's possession for over 800 years when it was sold in the 1950s) married Edward Jenner, the pioneer of inoculation, in 1788. A tablet in the porch records the event.

The A46 descends to Nailsworth, but the better route is to turn left for **Horsley**, following the B4058 downhill from that village. The church at Horsley was rebuilt by Thomas Richman who was largely responsible for the system of classification generally used for English church architecture.

Nailsworth has a thoroughly modern centre, but away from it there are some older, attractive houses, particularly in Market Street, where the eighteenth-century Clothiers Arms looks across to a row of very good cottages, and Stokes Croft, where one seventeenth-century house has an oval window (something of a local feature) in each of its three gables. Close by, the late seventeenth-century Quaker Meeting House is also very good. There are also good houses in Horsley Road. An attraction of an altogether different type is the Nailsworth Ladder, a road with the extreme gradient of 1 in 2.5. It has been used for hill-climbing events.

Nailsworth shop sign.

On the sides of the A46 beyond Nailsworth are a number of old cloth mills, some of which have been taken over by light industries. The Rooksmoor Mill is particularly noteworthy as it is now home to a craft potter, furniture showroom and small wine shop. Close to the mill is a left turn to **Woodchester**, famous for its Roman mosaic pavement. It seems that the existence of the pavement was known as early as 1695 when gravediggers unearthed part of it, though it was not thoroughly excavated for another hundred years. At 14m (46 ft) square it is the largest mosaic ever discovered in Britain and almost filled the room of the villa in which it was laid. The mosaic is also one of the finest, centred on Orpheus playing his lyre and featuring wild animals. After its first inspection the pavement was covered for a hundred years, then uncovered at irregular intervals, the last being in 1973. There are no plans for it to be uncovered in the immediate future.

From Woodchester, continue along the A46 to return to Stroud.

ADDRESSES AND OPENING TIMES

ROOKSMOOR MILL,
on the A46 south of Stroud *(01453 872577)*
❖
OPEN: all year, daily, 9.00am–5.00pm

OWLPEN MANOR,
near Uley *(01453 860261)*
❖
OPEN: April–Oct, Tues–Sun and
Bank Holiday Mon, 2.00–5.00pm;
restaurant open from 12.00am

THE HERITAGE CENTRE,
The Chipping, Wotton-under-Edge *(01453 521541)*
❖
OPEN: British Summer Time, Tues–Sat, 10.00am–1.00pm,
2.00–5.00pm
REMAINDER OF THE YEAR: Tues–Sat, 10.00am–1.00pm,
2.00–4.00pm

HORTON COURT (National Trust)
❖
OPEN: April–Oct, Wed and Sat, 2.00–4.00pm or sunset

WOODCHESTER MANSION,
near Nympsfield *(01453 860661)*
❖
OPEN: Easter Sat–Oct, Sat and Sun of 1st
weekend of month, 11.00am–4.00pm;
Sat, Sun and Mon of Bank Holiday weekends same times

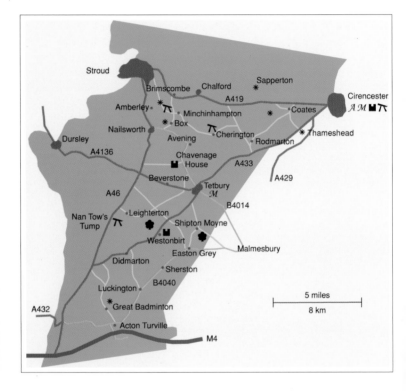

TOUR 8: The Golden Valley and Wold Villages

East of Stroud lies the Golden Valley named for the colour of its beech trees in autumn, rather than the wealth the mills on its river created for the wool workers in the heyday of the Cotswold trade – though that would seem just as appropriate. Many of the trees have gone now and the ribbon development of the valley, while not having blighted it (that would be an over-statement), has hardly enhanced its attractiveness. The valley is carved from the limestone plateau, the southern valley edge being Minchinhampton Common and its associated villages, an area of steep and confusingly intersecting roads guaranteed to confuse all but the most cautious.

From Stroud head eastwards along the A419, turning right at Bowbridge along a road that crosses river, canal and railway before climbing steeply to Butterow on Rodborough Common. The road passes an octagonal tollhouse where tolls were levied on coaches or animals moving up on to the Common. This list of charges is posted on a board on the front of the house.

At the Common is Rodborough Fort, an inhabited folly built by George Hawker in the mid-eighteenth century. Hawker apparently called it Fort George, but that name did not survive. Bear left and follow the road towards Minchinhampton, reaching a crossing of several roads at Long Tom's Post. The Long Tom of the name is not known, one local legend maintaining that he was a highwayman gibbeted at this spot so as to act as a deterrent, another stating that he was a suicide burial at the crossroads. This was customary: suicides were not allowed to be buried in consecrated ground, and it was believed that burial at a crossroads would confuse their inevitably restless spirits – not knowing which way to go, the spirit would go nowhere. From the Post, short detours are possible to three villages. **Amberley** is where Maria Craik wrote *John Halifax, Gentleman*: she lived at Rose Cottage. **Brimscombe**, back in the Golden Valley, was the

187

headquarters of the Thames and Severn Canal Company, and the old canal port and several mills can still be seen. **Box**, on the far side of Minchinhampton Common, has a church built in 1953, but in a traditional manner, with a Cotswold stone roof.

From the Post, go eastwards to reach **Minchinhampton**, passing the ramparts of The Bulwarks, a vast Iron Age hillfort covering over 240ha (600 acres). Minchinhampton was a very prosperous wool town, the local wolds producing fleeces of excellent quality. The Market House, supported on stone pillars, was built in 1698 and around it are gathered an array of fine seventeenth- and eighteenth-century merchants' houses. A contrast is offered by the Post Office which is in a delightful Queen Anne building. The church is instantly recognizable because of its truncated spire. The top section of the spire was dismantled in 1863 when it was in danger of collapse, the bottom section being capped by a coronet. The strange thing is why none of the town's clearly prosperous merchants felt inclined to build a new spire: there were certainly enough wealthy inhabitants, as a visit to the church will show. The south transept has a fine collection of effigies and tombs, and there are several brasses too. The effigies of a lady in the wimple and a knight (below the south window) are early fourteenth century and believed to be Sir Peter and Lady Matilda de la Mere. Look, too, for the brass of James Bradley, the Astronomer Royal, who died in 1762 (we met him at Sherborne).

From Minchinhampton go south-east to **Avening**, passing Gatcombe Park, on the right along the way. Avening has an early Norman church with some good memorials. Locally there are a number of long barrows, suggesting that the area was important in late Neolithic times. One of the best barrows is the Tingle Stone, where the stone of the name, the last remaining stone of a burial chamber, stands on top of the remnant earth mound. Legend has it that the stone runs around the field if it hears Avening church clock strike midnight. The name – which Earth Magic believers maintain derives from the sensation of touching the stone – is almost certainly from 'thing' the ancient Norse word for a meeting place, the root of, for instance, the Tynwald, the Isle of Man's Parliament. Three other burial chambers removed from local barrows were set in the hillside about 400m (440yd) north of the church in 1806, though quite why is a mystery (it was, perhaps, following a haphazard excavation of the barrows since a local legend maintained that they covered treasure). One of these has a rare port-hole entrance.

From Avening, head north-east to **Cherington**, where the green has a Victorian drinking fountain, continuing along minor roads through Tarlton, a pleasant little village, to reach Coates. The road crosses a filled section of the Thames and Severn Canal, and a short walk along that leads to the other end of the Sapperton Tunnel. Here, too, there is a bargees' inn. Fol-

Canal entrance, near Coates.

lowing the canal in the opposite direction from the road you will soon reach a tower-like Round House, one of many erected for the use of canal maintenance men. The canal can be followed to the ramparts of an Iron Age hillfort near Trewsbury House: turn right (south) beside the fort to follow a path to Thameshead, the official source of the River Thames. The statue of a reclining Neptune that once stood at the source was removed to Lechlade following vandalism. The source can also be reached by a path from the A433.

Coates is a well-spread, but attractive village. In the church, at the extreme western end, there is an unusual Norman font, with a cylindrical bowl at the top of a chamfered stem set on an octagonal base. From the village head south-eastwards to reach the A433 and turn right, soon passing the alternative path to

Thameshead. Just beyond, at Jackaments Bottom, Fosse Way leaves the A433, the main road bearing south-west towards Tetbury. Fosse Way heads through the Kemble Airfield (once, but no longer, home to the RAF's Red Arrows demonstration team). Soon, a turn right leads to **Rodmarton**, where there is a neat village green and spired church. Nearby is another long barrow, on Windmill Tump. From it a number of flint 'leaf' arrowheads were excavated (as well as several skeletons). The arrowheads are now in the British Museum. Further on, a left turn leads to Culkerton and Ashley, two quiet villages. Ahead now, the road leads to Tetbury.

Tetbury is a charming little market town with a splendid Market Hall at its heart. The Hall was built in 1655, its upper storey supported by fat Tuscan columns, and is often described as the best of its type in the Cotswolds. Until 1817 it must have been a remarkable building as in that year a second storey (or third if you count the open ground floor) was removed. Opposite the Hall is the seventeenth-century Snooty Fox, formerly the White Hart Inn. Go along Chipping Lane beside the inn to reach The Chipping, the old market, and some lovely old houses. In the

The Market Hall, Tetbury.

Tetbury on Woolsack race day.

north-west corner the large eighteenth-century house incorporates all that remains of Tetbury Priory. From the square, Chipping Steps lead down past delightful old houses. Equally steep is Gumstool Hill, which runs parallel to the steps, but from the Market Hall. The hill is named for the gum, or ducking, stool that once stood at the bottom. It is up the hill that, each Spring Bank Holiday, competitors run, carrying a 30kg (66lb) bale of wool, in one of the Cotswolds' most impressive annual events.

To the south of the Market Hall is St. Mary's Church, built only at the end of the eighteenth century despite the town's prosperous wool trade. The church has been described as the best example of Georgian Gothic in the country. The spire is 57m (186ft) tall, the fourth highest in England, and can be seen for miles around. Inside there are some good monuments and one intriguing one: which of the Saunders family lie below the tablet inscribed with the following verse?

'In a vault underneath
lie several of the Saunderses,

> late of this parish: particulars
> the Last Day will disclose.'

Equally intriguing is the reason for there being two churches at Tetbury. St. Mary's had a number of box pews which were 'owned' by the town's richest inhabitants. As the total number of pews was quite small, many of the poorer townsfolk were unable to find room when they came for Sunday services. The second church, St. Saviour's, in the appropriately named Newchurch Street was therefore built to accommodate them!

Heading west from the Market Hall, the visitor will pass a number of fine eighteenth- and nineteenth-century houses before reaching the town's old courthouse which now houses the Tourist Information Office and the Police Bygones Museum. The museum is housed in the old cells and has a collection of uniforms and equipment illustrating the history of the Gloucestershire constabulary.

To the west of Tetbury (follow the B4014 for Avening and turn left) is **Chavenage House**. The house was once owned by Horsley Priory, perhaps as a grange, and still has some fifteenth-century features (most notably the main staircase which has a stone newel), though most of what is now visible is Elizabethan from a comprehensive rebuilding by Sir Edward Stephens after the dissolution. The house is beautifully furnished, some seventeenth-century tapestries being particularly good, and is open to the public. Queen Anne's Room is where Princess Maria-Louise, a granddaughter of Queen Victoria, wrote *My Memories of Six Reigns*, but the best rooms are those named for Oliver Cromwell and Henry Ireton. It is claimed that the pair stayed at the house while persuading the owner, Colonel Nathaniel Stephens MP, of the need to execute Charles I. Although Stephens had been a Parliamentarian officer he was reluctant to support regicide, but eventually gave his support to the plan. Stephens died soon after the execution and apparently reputable sources claimed that after he had been laid in his coffin, a hearse drew up outside. That was no surprise, but it was then noticed that the driver of the hearse had no head. Stephens's corpse then rose from the coffin, walked to the hearse, bowed to the driver and climbed aboard. As the hearse rode away the onlookers realized that the driver was King Charles.

Also to the west of Tetbury, but on the A4135, is **Beverston**, where the most interesting items in the church are the wrought-iron light hangings made by the Tetbury blacksmith. The nearby castle is thirteenth century and was held for the King by a Colonel Oglethorpe. In 1644 it was attacked by Colonel Massey and a Parliamentarian force. Oglethorpe and his men put up a strong resistance and Massey, somewhat bruised, laid siege in the hope of forcing a surrender. Massey then discovered that a servant girl at Chavenage House was Oglethorpe's mistress and was passing information to him, Chavenage being staunchly for Parliament since Nathaniel Stephens owned it. When the girl heard that there was to be no attack on the castle that night she would place a candle in a certain window of the house and Oglethorpe would make his way through Massey's lines for a night of passion. Massey watched for the candle, arrested Oglethorpe and offered safe conduct to the castle troop if they surrendered. Appalled by their officer's conduct and capture, the troop did surrender, were allowed to go free and made their way eastwards to Malmesbury. There, a few days later, they were all captured when Massey, having secured Beverston, attacked the town.

From Tetbury, take the A433 southwards, soon turning left to **Shipton Moyne**. Just beyond the village, on the road to Malmesbury, the gardens at Hodges Barn are open to the public. The Barn belonged to a manor house which burned down in the sixteenth century. It, and a pair of dovecotes were converted into a house in 1938. The house gardens are typically English, with daffodils and bluebells in spring, and a mix of lawns and later-flowering shrubs. Before leaving the village, be sure to visit the church which has some splendid monuments. There are two effigies of knights in armour dating from the early fourteenth century and a number of very fine tombs of the Estcourt family.

Easton Grey.

Sherston.

From Shipton Moyne follow minor roads south-westwards to **Easton Grey**, just off the B4040, an extremely picturesque hamlet beside the River Avon, which is crossed by a stone, buttressed and arched bridge, probably dating from the sixteenth century. Now continue along the B4040 to **Sherston** where, legend has it, the Wessex king Edmund Ironsides and his general John Rattlebones defeated the Danes in 1016. An effigy in the church is said to be of Rattlebones, but is clearly Norman rather than Saxon. The church, which has an impressive, tall tower, was extended in 1730, the designer of the new building being paid the princely sum of £1.15 shillings. Continue along the B4040, passing an array of excellent seventeenth- and eighteenth-century houses, and then passing through Luckington to reach **Acton Turville** which has an old well topped by an iron portcullis on the green, and a fine old Toll House, both from the early nineteenth century. In the village turn right for Badminton.

The village of **Great Badminton** lies beside Badminton Park, one of the great estates of Britain, home of the Beauforts, and also of the world-famous Three-Day Event, a highlight of the equestrian calendar. Badminton House dates from the early sixteenth century when Edward Somerset, Earl of Worcester, bought the estate, though it took thirty years to build. In 1682 the incumbent Worcester was

194

made the first Duke of Beaufort. Inside the house there are some of Grinling Gibbons's major works. Though it is not known who was responsible for the house, it was Capability Brown who remodelled the parkland. The park covers 6,000ha (15,000 acres) and has one of Britain's finest avenues, Great Avenue, which runs southwards for almost 5km (3 miles) from Worcester Lodge (on the A433 near Didmarton) to the northern entrance of the House. St. Michael's Church, within the estate, has an array of fine monuments to members of the Beaufort dynasty, most notably that by Grinling Gibbons of the first Duke, who died in 1699.

The village beside the park consists of estate workers' cottages and an interesting group of early eighteenth-century almshouses. Follow the road from the village around the boundary of the park, going through Little Badminton and continuing to the A46. Turn right, and soon right again along the A433, passing Worcester Lodge, on the right, to reach **Didmarton** which has several good eighteenth- and nineteenth-century houses. Rather than restore the village's medieval church (to St. Lawrence), the Victorians built another (to St. Michael). St. Lawrence's is, therefore, a rather good example of the way most medieval churches looked in the late eighteenth century. Continue along the A433 to reach **Westonbirt**.

There is a village here, to the right from the main road, though the main interest is in Westonbirt House, built in the 1860s for Robert Holford. The house was built in a sixteenth-century style and is magnificent, as are the Italian gardens. The church houses Holford's tomb, on which he lays in effigy, splendidly robed in ermine. Westonbirt House is now a girls' school, but it and the gardens are open to visitors on one day each year. Ask at Tetbury's Tourist Information Office or ring the school for details.

Across the main road from the village is the world-famous Westonbirt Arboretum. The Arboretum was begun by Robert Holford – the builder of the House – in 1829 when he was just twenty-one years old, one of the reasons being his desire for a

Autumnal full moon at Westonbirt Arboretum.

beautiful park to view from the House. Holford's original
design was courageous: he left rides almost 20m (60ft) wide
between the tree groups, knowing that for many years they
would be far from elegant. Holford died in 1892, by which time
his decision had been vindicated. The Forestry Commission
acquired the Arboretum in 1956 and it is now run by Forest
Enterprise, an arm of the Commission. To attempt a description of the site would be to fail: it covers 240ha (600 acres) and
is planted with almost 20,000 trees from many hundreds of
species. It would be equally difficult to suggest when to visit:
in spring the azaleas and magnolias are in bloom, and there are
wild flowers in Silk Wood; in summer the trees are in full
foliage; in autumn the red, golds and browns are beautiful,
especially among the acers; even in winter the Arboretum is
beautiful, particularly if there has been a frost to highlight the
coloured bark of birch and dogwood. The Arboretum also has
a range of special events: in autumn coloured lights are strung
between the trees and evening walks are magical, and at

Christmas, Father Christmas occupies a woodland grotto. A full programme of special events is given in the Visitor Centre. The Arboretum also has a picnic site and a plant centre where trees and shrubs may be bought.

Continue along the A433 to Tetbury, taking the B4014 from there to Nailsworth, and returning to Stroud along the A46.

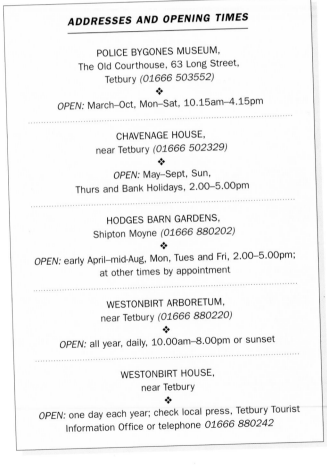

ADDRESSES AND OPENING TIMES

POLICE BYGONES MUSEUM,
The Old Courthouse, 63 Long Street,
Tetbury *(01666 503552)*
❖
OPEN: March–Oct, Mon–Sat, 10.15am–4.15pm

CHAVENAGE HOUSE,
near Tetbury *(01666 502329)*
❖
OPEN: May–Sept, Sun,
Thurs and Bank Holidays, 2.00–5.00pm

HODGES BARN GARDENS,
Shipton Moyne *(01666 880202)*
❖
OPEN: early April–mid-Aug, Mon, Tues and Fri, 2.00–5.00pm;
at other times by appointment

WESTONBIRT ARBORETUM,
near Tetbury *(01666 880220)*
❖
OPEN: all year, daily, 10.00am–8.00pm or sunset

WESTONBIRT HOUSE,
near Tetbury
❖
OPEN: one day each year; check local press, Tetbury Tourist
Information Office or telephone *01666 880242*

TOUR 9: Badminton to Bath

Bath is the obvious centre for a tour of the Southwolds that lie to the south of the M4 (with one short trip north of the motorway, to Tormarton). Bath is also the southern extremity of the AONB, which finishes on the hills at the city's southern edge, and also at the southern limit of the geological area which defines the Cotswolds, the Cotswold scarp slope falling into the River Avon. So, despite the title, this final tour of the AONB will go northwards to the M4, not southwards from it.

From Bath take the A431 towards Bitton. The road runs past the suburban village of Weston (where the Cotswold Way enters the city on its way to its end at Bath Abbey) then continues to **Kelston**, where the church houses a fragment of a Saxon cross shaft. Kelston Park was the work of John Wood the Younger. Beyond, a steep road on the right reaches **North Stoke**, a very pleasant village. Significant Roman remains have been excavated from sites near the village. Continue along the A431, taking the next right turn to reach Upton Cheney. Go through the village, bearing right to follow a road uphill on to the northern end of Lansdown. At the crossroads, turn right, still climbing, and go around a long right-hand bend to reach the **Granville Monument** on the left.

On 5 July 1643 the Parliamentarian governor of Bath, Sir William Waller, took up a position here on the northern end of Lansdown in order to prevent a large Royalist army from attacking the city. Waller mounted artillery at the edge of the hill and then attacked the Royalists who were at the bottom of the slope. In what was probably a mock retreat to draw the Royalists up the hill, Waller's men ran up the hill, the pursuing Royalist being met with withering cannon fire. Just as it seemed that the Royalists would be routed, Sir Bevil Granville, the leader of a group of Cornishmen, led his men up the hill, riding his horse across the slope to encourage the advance. The Cornishmen took the Parliamentarian position, but at the moment of victory Sir Bevil was mortally wounded. The Roundheads retreated and took up a position behind a wall, but the tired Royalists did not follow. During the night Waller's men lit camp fires, but then retreated to the city, the morning light showing the Royalists that they had been duped. It took two more weeks of fighting before the Royalists finally took the city. The monument to Sir Bevil, a huge and somewhat ungainly structure, was erected by his grandson Lord Lansdown. To the south of the monument is Bath racecourse, built on Lansdown's flat top. The Cotswold Way runs between the course and the scarp edge, eventually reaching Prospect Stile, one of its most famous viewpoints, the sight of Kelston Round Hill telling walkers that their journey to Bath is almost at an end.

From the monument, return down the hill but, on the crown of the long bend, bear right, following a minor road to the A420. Turn right to reach a roundabout and, from there, make a short detour to **Cold Ashton** by going right, towards Bath, then left into the village. It was to the Manor House here (a beautiful Elizabethan house, often maintained to be the best example of the period in England) that Sir Bevil was brought after being wounded at Lansdown and where he died. The village church is also worth a visit. It was built entirely at the expense of the vicar Thomas Key, explaining the symbol of an intertwined key and T which may be seen in several places.

Continue through the village to regain the A420 and turn right towards **Marshfield**, turning right again to reach the village. Marshfield's name almost certainly derives, as with Moreton-in-Marsh, from its being on the border between Wessex and Mercia. To the south-east of the

Marshfield.

village there is also a stone that marked the point where Gloucestershire, Somerset and Wiltshire met before the redrawing of county boundaries. The village consists of little more than the High Street, at the eastern end of which is St. Mary's Church, a fine Perpendicular structure built in the late fifteenth century. The village's position, at the highest point for many miles, and the height of the tower make it a well-known landmark. Moving west along the High Street, the visitor passes several fine eighteenth-century inns, built because of the village's proximity to Bath. The Tolzey Hall bears a strange inscription stating that it was built in 1690, but removed and rebuilt in 1793. Where had it been and why was it moved? At the western end of the village are the Crispe Almshouses, built in the early seventeenth century by Elias Crispe for eight poor village folk. With their gables and central clock tower and spire the houses are quite charming.

From Marshfield, follow a minor road north-westwards to **West Littleton**, which has a good sixteenth-century manor house, and on to the A46. To the left from here is **Dyrham Park**.

Dyrham Park.

The *Anglo-Saxon Chronicle* relates that in 577 Cuthwine and Ceawlin fought against the Britons and killed three kings, Conmail, Condidan and Farinmail, at the place called Dyrham, and captured three of their cities, Gloucester, Cirencester and Bath. The Saxons heading westwards across England had taken up a position in the Iron Age hillfort on Hinton Hill, just north of Dyrham. They were attacked by the local Celts (Britons) who were routed. The Saxons had succeeded in splitting Britain in half, isolating the West Country Celts from those in Wales and the north. This isolation made the Saxon job of securing England much easier: soon the Celts had been pushed into the sea in Cornwall and contained behind Offa's Dyke.

Dyrham Park does not include Hinton Hill, though it may be visited along the Cotswold Way which follows the hill's southern flank to reach Dyrham village. The house in Dyrham Park was built by William Blathwayt, Secretary of State for War under William III, in about 1700, the Baroque mansion having at its heart the Great Hall from the previous Tudor mansion on the site. The interior of the house is virtually unchanged from Blathwayt's time (as his housekeeper's inventory confirms). The house stands in over 100ha (250 acres) of parkland which Blathwayt kept as a deer park (a herd of fallow deer still occupies it), but also had built what was then considered the finest water garden in Britain, with a dammed lake feeding fountains, a cascade, and creating a 6m (20ft) water jet. Sadly the system had become ruinous within a hundred years. The Park and House are now administered by the National Trust.

The village church, beside the Park, has a superb brass to Sir Maurice Russell and his wife, dating from the late fourteenth century and so similar to the Berkeley brasses at Wotton-under-Edge that it is believed to be the work of the same craftsman.

From Dyrham, head north along the A46, crossing the M4 and then turning right to **Tormarton**, a delightful little village with a church showing both Saxon and early Norman features. Inside there is a fine brass to John Ceysill who died in 1493. Ceysill was the steward of Tormarton's rector and is shown with his pen and inkhorn. Look, too, for the memorial to Edward Topp which shows a mailed fist clutching a severed arm.

Take the minor road southwards from Tormarton, going above the M4 to reach a crossroads. Turn left and follow the road to the B4039, turning right into **Burton** where the church is one of the 'Wiltshire Group' of five churches that show a distinctive form of the Perpendicular style. Burton's church tower is often claimed to be the best in Wiltshire. To the south of the village a short detour reaches Nettleton, a scattered village, and **West Kington**, whose church is another of the Wiltshire Group. Hugh Latimer was the vicar here before becoming Bishop of Worcester. Latimer was one of several bishops who were burnt at the stake for refusing to accept Roman Catholicism during the reign of Mary Tudor.

From Burton, follow the B4039 eastwards to reach a turning, on the right, for **Castle Combe**, a village as perfect as any in the

northern Cotswolds, and by far the loveliest in the Southwolds. The hill spur above Bay Brook was occupied by the Romans, as it was a convenient spot close to Fosse Way which could be used as both a staging and a guard post. The Romans also built the first bridge over the brook, a bridge now reputedly haunted by a centurion. Medieval Castle Combe was a wool village, one pair of village brothers, the Blankets, being said to have invented the article

stle Combe.

203

which now bears their name. The village was also home to Sir John Fastolf, a lord of the manor on whom Shakespeare is said to have based his character Falstaff.

The visitor using the village car park – and there is little choice – reaches the main village street (The Street) at the Market and Butter Crosses. The fine pyramidal Market Cross is fourteenth century, while all that remains of the Butter Cross is a small pile of stones where the old Market Hall once stood. To the right, Archway Cottage was once the gatehouse of the manor house, the house now being a hotel. Ahead is the village church, opposite a row of beautiful old cottages. The church has an interesting effigy of a knight above niche figures of six mourners. The knight is Walter de Dunstanville who was killed in 1270. It is believed that the mourners, three men and three women, are his children.

From the crosses, bear left down The Street. The half-timbered house on the left is fifteenth century and was once the courthouse. Beyond, to both left and right there are beautiful old houses. Among the best are the weavers' cottages on the left by the old packhorse bridge over By Brook. The house at the end of the cottages it that of the Master Weaver. That part of Castle Combe by the bridge is exquisite and was used for the filming of *Dr Dolittle*, when it was converted into a small port.

From Castle Combe, continue along the B4039 to **Yatton Keynell** where there is another of the five Wiltshire Group churches. The church was built by Sir William Keynell in thanks to his safe return from a crusade and is dedicated to St. Margaret of Antioch who, he believed, had safeguarded him. From the village head south to reach the A420. To the south is **Biddestone**, an exquisite place, its houses grouped around a green and a pond. It is the last village in the AONB to be built of what may be correctly termed Cotswold stone. Turn right along the A420, soon reaching **Ford**, a pleasantly sited village with some nice houses. To the south from here is **Slaughterford**, named, as with the Slaughter villages to the north, for its sloes rather than a battle, while a little further along the A420 and to the right is **North Wraxall**, whose thirteenth-century church has a much earlier Norman doorway. On nearby Truckle Hill a Roman villa has been excavated and found to be lying within an enclosure. Perhaps the natives were not that friendly after all.

From Ford take the minor road to **Colerne**, famous for its air-field, and for its church, which is a landmark for miles around. There are fragments of a ninth-century Saxon cross in the church: it is said that the cross was erected at a stopping place of the procession carrying St. Aldhelm's body to Malmesbury. Much later the village was famous for its beers, the local fields growing fine barley. On a less happy note, Hitching's Skilling remembers the execution of a Crimean War deserter.

To the south, a return to Bath can be made along the A4 via Box, well-known to railway enthusiasts for its tunnel on the GWR line. Box Tunnel is 2,940m (3,212yd) long and was built, between 1837 and 1841 by I.K. Brunel. It is said that Brunel oriented the tunnel so that on his birthday the rising sun would shine along it. Chapel Plaister, a short distance to the south-east of the village, is named for a hospice built in the fifteenth century to house pilgrims on their way to Glastonbury.

But a better way to return to Bath, rather than through Box, is to head westwards along the minor road past Colerne air-field to reach a T-junction with Fosse Way. To the left from here is the **Three Shires Stone** constructed to look like a dol-men, the burial chamber of a long barrow. Take the road opposite, following as it winds down into St. Catherine's Val-ley. The village of **St. Catherine** is reached at a T-junction: turn right to reach St. Catherine's Court. The Court is a beautiful building, constructed in the late fifteenth century as a Bene-dictine monastery, then modified after the dissolution. It was given by Henry VIII to his tailor John Malte, in exchange (it is said) for Malte's having adopted or become the guardian, of an illegitimate daughter fathered by Henry with one of the Court's ladies-in-waiting.

From St. Catherine's, head southwards along the valley to reach the A4 at **Batheaston**, where there are some excellent eighteenth-century houses and a good church with a tall tower. Across the valley from the village Little Solsbury Hill is topped by an Iron Age hillfort. To the south of the village is **Bathford**, where there are also excellent eighteenth-century houses. In the woods above the village is Brown's Folly, a tower built in 1840 by Wade Brown. When asked why he had built it he answered, somewhat enigmatically, that it was for surveying reasons. To the east of Bathford, the AONB's final village is **Monkton Farleigh**, its steep streets leading to a fine Gothic Rectory, built in 1844. The Manor House was built around the remains of a twelfth-century Cluniac priory.

From the bottom of the St. Catherine's Valley, where the road reaches the A4, turn right to return to Bath.

ADDRESS AND OPENING TIMES

DYRHAM PARK (National Trust)
(0117 937 2501)

❖

PARK: open all year, daily, 12.00am–5.30pm or dusk
(open at 11.00am on days garden is open)
GARDEN: open Easter–Oct, Fri–Tues, 11.00am–5.30pm
HOUSE: open Easter–Oct, Fri–Tues, 12.00am–5.30pm

King Bladud, Cross Bath.

Bath

At the King's Bath and Cross Bath, two of the city's spas, there are statues of Bladud, the inscription declaring him to have been the son of Hudibras, the eighth King of the Britons. He was, it says, a philosopher and mathematician and had been born in Athens. Most significantly he is said to be the founder of Bath in 863BC.

BATH

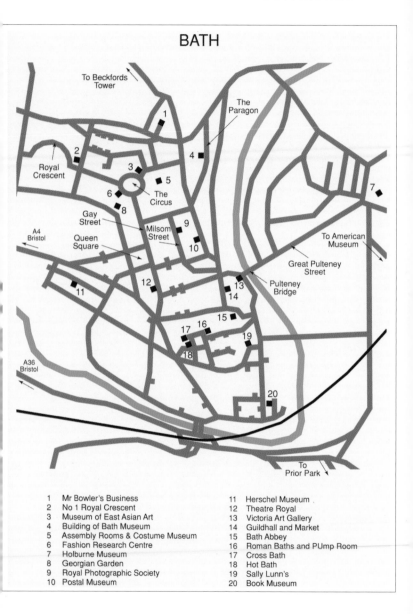

To Beckfords Tower

The Paragon

Royal Crescent

The Circus

Gay Street

A4 Bristol

Queen Square

Milsom Street

To American Museum

Great Pulteney Street

Pulteney Bridge

A36 Bristol

To Prior Park

1   Mr Bowler's Business
2   No 1 Royal Crescent
3   Museum of East Asian Art
4   Building of Bath Museum
5   Assembly Rooms & Costume Museum
6   Fashion Research Centre
7   Holburne Museum
8   Georgian Garden
9   Royal Photographic Society
10 Postal Museum
11 Herschel Museum
12 Theatre Royal
13 Victoria Art Gallery
14 Guildhall and Market
15 Bath Abbey
16 Roman Baths and PUmp Room
17 Cross Bath
18 Hot Bath
19 Sally Lunn's
20 Book Museum

Bladud, son of Hudibras, was descended from the Trojans, one of whom, fleeing Agamemnon in the wake of the siege of Troy, came to Britain and gathered a kingdom that covered the southern part of the country. Bladud contracted leprosy and was banished from his father's court, becoming a swineherd in the north of what is now Somerset. He infected his pigs and moved them to a wild part of the country where, he hoped, they would all die peacefully, away from the prejudiced eyes of his father's people. The pigs liked the new country, finding warm mud pools in which to wallow and, to Bladud's amazement, their leprosy was cured. Bladud, too, covered himself with the mud and to his joy was also cured. He returned to his father's court, taking his rightful place as heir to the throne. When his father died, Bladud moved the court to the place of the warm mud pools, which he called Aquae Sulis, the Waters of the Sun. As King he travelled to Athens to learn at the feet of the great philosophers, dying there when the wings that he had invented failed to live up to his expectations during his maiden flight from the top of a tall temple. Back in Britain, Bladud was succeeded by his son Lear, about whom a later Englishman, one William Shakespeare, wrote a play.

Bladud's warm pools were fed by several hundred thousand gallons of water daily, the water erupting from the ground at 50°C (120°F). It is probably true that the first Britons who arrived at what is now Bath knew of the water, but it was the Romans, to whom hot water springs were a gift from the gods, who first exploited them. After Hadrian's Wall, Bath is probably the best known Roman site in Britain.

It was actually the Romans who named the town Aquae Sulis, building a temple to Sul Minerva near to their main bath (the one which visitors can still explore) – standing close to the Abbey. One of the finest items to have been excavated from the area is a head of Sul, the Celtic sun god, showing all the ferocity of the Celts and proving, yet again, that Rome maintained its empire by a combination of the short sword and a clever incorporation of local beliefs into a Roman framework.

Another interesting item is the 'Bath curse', a lead sheet inscribed by a jilted lover: 'May he who took Vilbia from me become water', and listing the nine likeliest culprits.

Roman Bath seems to have been experiencing problems from a rising water table in the third century AD, but within a hundred years the problems had become academic: the Romans had gone anyway, leaving the town to decay. The Saxons noticed the ruins, but the standard of the building was so advanced compared with their own that they thought it was an old town of the gods. As a consequence, Bath became a sacred place, even though the Saxons made no attempt to utilize the warm springs, or even to build much of a town. In about 760 King Offa founded an abbey, and in 973 Edgar was crowned there, becoming the first true King of England.

Following the Norman conquest, Bath was almost destroyed in the conflict between William Rufus and his barons. To provide a boost to the area, the Bishop of Bath and Wells moved his seat to the town. He began a new church and, most importantly, promoted the healing qualities of the waters. Unfortunately, those who came were the poor folk, those who could not afford doctors. By the time John Leland, the Elizabethan traveller, visited Bath in 1533 the baths stank and were a health hazard rather than a cure. Hoping to increase the appeal of the waters, the town cleaned up the baths and was rewarded by visits from Queen Elizabeth I, Queen Anne, the wife of James I, and Charles I and Queen Henrietta Maria. The Civil War brought a halt to its growing prosperity, but then, in 1705, the man who was to make Bath's fortune arrived. Richard 'Beau' Nash was Swansea-born and had enjoyed a colourful life by the time he was appointed the official Master of Ceremonies by the town corporation. Nash had already shown a talent for organization and at Bath this talent blossomed into genius. He ran the town (and 'ran' is the correct term, nothing much happening without his consent or involvement) for over fifty years, almost until his death in 1761 at the age of eighty-seven. In thanks, the city erected a statue to him in the Pump Room.

Under Nash, Bath became the social centre of Britain, its afflu-ence triggering a building boom which has left the city with the finest array of Georgian buildings in the country, a legacy of the work of Ralph Allen and the John Woods, father and son.

Allen was the Cornishman responsible for taking the British postal system, at the time an unprofitable business routing all mail through London despite the delays that caused, and turn-ing it into an efficient organization that was a necessity rather than a tiresome luxury. With the fortune he made he bought the quarries from which Bath stone was cut. The older John Wood, a Yorkshireman, was the architect whose work with Allen's stone transformed Bath into a city as elegant as Beau Nash's clientele.

Nash's Bath was an endless round of socializing. There were morning and afternoon walks along defined promenades, the waters were taken, the theatres and concerts were enjoyed, dances were attended and, best of all for many, there was gam-bling. It all continued after Nash's death, but the loss of his inventiveness, together with boredom over the sameness of it all, meant that Bath became *passé*. By 1800 the boom was over, though the huge wealth Bath had gained allowed it to make the transition into an industrial town with relative ease. Late-ly the city has rediscovered its Roman and Georgian heritage and has become one of the West Country's leading tourist cen-tres. It can be crowded almost to the point of choking on occa-sions, but the sheer range of its attractions – architectural as well as the more formal museums and galleries, and some good parks too – means that in the main it can absorb the visitors.

A full exploration of Bath would require its own book. Below we explore the heart of the city, taking in the major Georgian buildings and the Roman baths. Bath is a city of museums and galleries, many of them among the finest of their type in the country: those that lie on the suggested walk-ing tour are noted, but all the sites are listed and the relevant information on each is given.

Any tour of Bath should start at the Abbey. The present building is the third on the site, following a Saxon church

Bath Abbey viewed from the Roman Baths.

constructed in 781 and a huge Norman cathedral, built in 1107. The present church was begun in 1499 by Oliver King, Bishop of Bath and Wells. King had a dream in which he saw angels climbing ladders to heaven and heard a voice saying, 'Let a King restore the church'. The Abbey's beautiful west front has the figures of angels scaling the ladders of the dream. Inside the church is wonderfully light and airy, Bishop King having made full use of the new techniques for improving the size of windows. The monuments include those of Beau Nash in the south aisle and, nearby, that of Lady Waller, the wife of the Parliamentary governor of the city. Look, too, for the huge monument to James Montague, an early seventeenth-century Bishop of Bath and Wells. But good though the monuments are, the highlight of the interior is the chantry chapel of William Birde, its stonework so intricate that it bankrupted its benefactor. The Heritage Vaults are reached from the south aisle, by the Choir.

From the Abbey, cross the square outside the main entrance (in the west front), passing the Roman Baths and Pump Room to the left, bear left (to the entrance to the Baths complex) and then bear right along Bath Street to reach the Cross Bath, ahead, and the Hot Bath, to the left. The colonnade in Bath Street was to protect patrons of the Cross Bath from the weather. The cross of Cross Bath's name was erected after the supposedly infertile Queen Mary, the wife of James II, conceived following her use of the bath. It has since been removed. The Hot Bath is the work of John Wood's son (also called John, the two now being distinguished by being 'the Elder' and 'the Younger'). It was built in 1773 and now houses an art gallery.

Bear left and right to reach Westgate Buildings. Turn right, bearing right along Sawclose to pass the Theatre Royal on the left. Just before it, the bust of Beau Nash marks the site of his house, while just beyond a plaque indicates the home of his mistress Juliana Popjoy, where Nash spent his last years. Walk straight ahead along Burton Street, and then along the eastern edge of Queen Square, named after Queen Caroline, the wife of George II. The Square was the first work of

Popjoy's Restaurant, Bath.

John Wood the Elder. Wood lived in the Square, dying here in 1754. Another resident was Dr Oliver, inventor of the Bath Oliver biscuit. The obelisk was raised by Beau Nash in memory of Prince Frederick.

Continue straight up Gay Street, named for the surgeon who owned the land on which it was built. John Wood the Younger lived here. Turn left along the Queen's Parade Place. To the left is where Bath's sedan chairmen would wait for fares, a Georgian taxi-rank. Continue to the steps on the right and go up them to the Georgian Garden. Lovers of Jane Austen will recognize the gravel walk here as being the place Captain Wentworth and Anne Elliot declared their mutual love in *Persuasion*. The Garden has been restored to its original 1700 plan, using plants from a Webb's catalogue of that year. Follow the walk to its end, then bear left to Royal Crescent.

Royal Crescent, Bath.

The Crescent was John Wood the Younger's masterpiece, the first crescent in the world and still the finest. It has thirty houses and 114 Ionic columns and, with the lawns and park at its front, is the epitome of elegance. No.1 is now a museum, and it was from No.11 that Elizabeth Linley and Richard Brinsley Sheridan eloped.

After admiring the Crescent, go along Brock Street to reach The Circus, John Wood the Elder's masterpiece (but completed by his son, after the father had died). It has three groups of eleven houses with Doric, Ionic and Corinthian columns on the three floors. The street was Britain's first circle and was inspired by Rome's Colosseum and the stone circles of what was then still believed to be Druidic Britain. The acorn symbols at the tops of the houses are a reminder of the Druids' sacred oak groves.

The Circus, Bath

Walk through The Circus to Bennett Street, passing the Museum of East Asian Art on the left, and turning right almost immediately to walk beside the Assembly Rooms, which now house the Museum of Costume. Turn left along Alfred Street (named for King Alfred whose bust may be seen to the right), following it to The Paragon, another superb collection of houses. Jane Austen lived at No.1 during her visits to her uncle and aunt in 1797. When she took up residence in Bath she lived in Sydney Place, further along the route. The Paragon's Gothic chapel now houses the Buildings of Bath Museum. Next door is the Schoolhouse Gallery.

Turn right along The Paragon, bearing right along George Street to reach the top of Milsom Street on the left. Go down Milsom Street, passing Shire's Yard on your left. Here stands the Postal Museum. A few steps beyond is The Octagon, the Royal Photographic Society's gallery. At the bottom of Milsom Street, walk ahead to reach Trim Street, on the right and New Bond Street on the left. General Wolfe, the victor of Quebec, lived at No.5 Trim Street. Turn left along New Bond Street, then bear right and left into Bridge Street. To the right as you reach Bridge Street is the Guildhall, while at the end of the street, to the right, is the Victorian Art Gallery.

Ahead now is Pulteney Bridge, one of the most picturesque buildings in the town. The bridge was built in 1769 by Robert

Adam, and, clearly inspired by Florence's Ponte Vecchio, is one of few now left in Europe to retain shops on both sides. It is named for Sir William Pulteney, the bridge linking his estate to Georgian Bath. The weir below the bridge was built in 1971 to prevent flooding and is popular with canoeists.

Beyond the bridge a long detour follows Argyle Street/Great Pulteney Street to the Holburne Museum, seen at the end of these long, straight thoroughfares. Close to the museum, at No.4 Sydney Place, is the house where Jane Austen lived during her stay in Bath.

From the city end of the bridge, go along Grand Parade, passing Orange Grove on the right and the Parade Gardens on the left, to reach North Parade on the left. William Wordsworth and Oliver Goldsmith lived in the Parade, while in Pierrepoint Street, ahead, Lord Nelson lived with Lady Emma Hamilton. In Old Orchard Street, reached through the arch from Pierrepoint Street, stands Linley House. It was here that Emma Hart was a servant before she became Lady Hamilton. The House is named for the musician Thomas Linley, whose daughter Elizabeth eloped with Sheridan.

Turn right at North Parade to go along North Parade Passage, passing Sally Lunn's on the right. Continue along North Parade

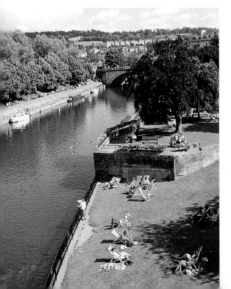

Passage, then turn right along Church Street, crossing York Street, where Ralph Allen lived in a house designed by John Wood the Elder. Continue along Church Street to return to the Abbey, a fitting place to end the tour of both the city and the Cotswolds.

The River Avon, Bath.

Sites on the Walking Tour

Heritage Vaults, Bath Abbey

The ecclesiastical history of Bath is explored in the vaults below the Abbey. The collection includes carvings from both the Saxon and Norman churches that formerly stood on the Abbey site.

Roman Baths and Pump Room

The baths are the finest example of Roman domestic architecture in the country. The Great Bath, overshadowed by the Abbey, is the most impressive and still fills with the hot water that brought the Romans to the site. There are also smaller baths and a Temple to Sul Minerva, the goddess of wisdom and healing. The site includes a museum of excavated objects which are a graphic illustration of life in this section of Roman Bath. Most striking is the famous Head of Sul.

The Pump Room was the centre of Georgian Bath's social life and has items relating to the period – a statue of Beau Nash and a sedan chair being among the most interesting. Visitors can take tea where the socialites mingled, or sample the spa water to the accompaniment of the Pump Room Trio.

Hot Bath Gallery

The Gallery specializes in the work of local artists, but also has occasional exhibitions by other British or international artists.

No.1 Royal Crescent

The house, first occupied by John Wood the Younger's father-in-law and later by George II's son the Duke of York, is now a museum to Georgian Bath. It has been beautifully restored and is furnished in period style. There is also a collection that really brings the era alive.

Museum of East Asian Art

The Museum specializes in work from China, Japan, Korea and other countries of south-east Asia and has a beautiful collection exploring the development of art in that area from 5,000BC to the present day.

Assembly Rooms/Museum of Costume

The Assembly Rooms were the work of John Wood the Younger, replacing an earlier building that had been outgrown. In

Georgian times the Rooms were where ladies took tea and gentlemen gambled. There was also a ballroom. The beautiful decoration of the rooms is worth the visit, but they now also house
the Museum of Costume, one of the finest of its type in the
world, which explores the development of men's, women's and
children's clothing from the late sixteenth century to the present.

The Fashion Research Centre, part of the Museum of Costume, with a library and study centre on the history of fashion, is at No.4 The Circus.

Buildings of Bath Museum

Housed in the Countess of Huntington's Chapel, built in
Gothic style in 1765 as a non-conformist chapel, the Museum
explores both the building and the buildings of Georgian
Bath. There is also an interesting collection of British folk art.

Schoolhouse Gallery

Next door to the Buildings of Bath Museum, the Gallery has
exhibitions of both local and national artists with a bias towards
architectural themes.

Postal Museum

From this museum the first letter bearing a postage stamp, a
'penny black', was sent on 2 May 1840. The museum includes
a reconstructed Victorian post office, and a collection exploring the development of postal services from earliest times.

Royal Photographic Society Gallery

Housed in the Octagon Chapel (William Herschel was once
the organist in this private chapel) is the collection of the RPS
with some very early and rare items. The Gallery also has regular exhibitions by leading photographers.

Guildhall

The Guildhall was built in 1776 and has what is widely regarded as the finest Adam-style interior in Britain. The Banqueting Room on the first floor is magnificent. It is lit by a crystal
chandelier of 1778 and hung with portraits of some of the
famous people associated with Bath.

Victoria Art Gallery

The Gallery is divided into two: The Upper Gallery has a

permanent collection of British and European art from the fifteenth to the twentieth century. The eighteenth- and nineteenth-century works are arguably the finest part of the collection, with paintings by Gainsborough and Turner among others. The Lower Gallery has temporary exhibitions.

Holburne Museum and Crafts Study Centre
Housed in a former hotel is the collection of Sir William Holburne (1793–1874), with silver, porcelain, glass, furniture and paintings. Since Holburne's death the collection has been enlarged, particularly with some fine paintings by Gainsborough and Stubbs. The Crafts Study Centre has work by contemporary craft workers.

Sally Lunn's
Sally Lunn's claims to be Bath's oldest house. It is named for a French refugee who opened a tea shop in the 1680s and became famous and prosperous because of the bun that now bears her name. The house is still a tea shop and still sells the buns, but there is also a museum in the cellars. Here sections of Roman and medieval buildings can be seen, together with the original kitchen and a collection of old cooking utensils.

Sites Outside the City Centre

American Museum
Situated at Claverton, to the east of the city. The museum, in Claverton Manor, explores the history of North America from the Pilgrim Fathers to more recent times, with rooms in period American furniture. There are collections on the native Americans and on the West.

Beckford's Tower
Situated on the south-eastern end of Lansdown, to the northwest of the city. The 47m (154ft) Italianate tower was erected by William Beckford, a wealthy traveller and collector. It offers a fine view of the local area, though not such a good one of the city, and houses a museum of items on Beckford, particularly of the lavish Fonthill Abbey which the architect James Wyatt built for him on his Wiltshire estate.

Book Museum

Situated in Manvers Street, the continuation of Pierrepoint Street. The Museum has a fascinating collection exploring the history of bookbinding, together with items on Bath in literature, with rare books and prints.

William Herschel Museum

The home of William Herschel in New King Street, a short distance to the west of Queen Square. It was while living in this house that Herschel discovered the planet Uranus in 1781 using one of the telescopes he built as a hobby. He later became Astronomer Royal. The Museum has a collection of memorabilia on Herschel's life as a musician (he was organist at the Octagon Chapel) and astronomer.

Mr Bowler's Business

The marvellous alternative name for the Bath Industrial Heritage Centre, housed in a reconstruction of Mr J.B. Bowler's brass foundry and fizzy-drink factory. The centre, in Julian Road a short distance to the north of the Assembly Rooms, also explores the life of the ordinary inhabitants of the city at the height of its Georgian prosperity.

Prior Park Landscaped Garden

Situated to the south-east of the city, and above it. The Park is an eighteenth-century garden financed by Ralph Allen and landscaped by Capability Brown. It is complete with typical sham buildings, grotto and lake. The National Trust has restored the Park, which had fallen into disrepair. There are also several miles of woodland walking. The views of the city are breathtaking.

ADDRESSES AND OPENING TIMES

HERITAGE VAULTS,
Bath Abbey *(01225 422462)*
❖
OPEN: all year, Mon–Sat, 10.00am–4.00pm

ROMAN BATHS/PUMP ROOM,
Stall Street *(01225 477785)*

❖

OPEN: April–Oct, Mon–Sat, 9.00am–6.00pm,
Sun 10.00am–5.30pm;
Oct–March, Mon–Sat, 9.30am–5.00pm,
Sun 10.30am–5.00pm;
daily in Aug, 8.00am–10.00pm

HOT BATH GALLERY,
Hotbath Street *(01225 328673)*

❖

OPEN: all year, Mon–Thurs, 10.00am–7.00pm,
Fri and Sat 10.00am–4.00pm

NO.1 ROYAL CRESCENT
(01225 428126)

❖

OPEN: mid Feb–Oct, Tues–Sun and Bank Holiday Mon,
10.30am–5.00pm;
Nov, Tues–Sun, 10.30am–4.00pm

MUSEUM OF EAST ASIAN ART,
12 Bennett Street *(01225 464640)*

❖

OPEN: April–Oct, Mon–Sat, 10.00am–6.00pm,
Sun 10.00am–5.00pm;
Nov–March, Mon–Sat, 10.00am–5.00pm,
Sun 12.00am–5.00pm

ASSEMBLY ROOMS/MUSEUM OF COSTUME,
Bennett Street *(01225 477785)*

❖

OPEN: all year, Mon–Sat, 10.00am–5.00pm,
Sun 11.00am–5.00pm

FASHION RESEARCH CENTRE,
4 The Circus *(01225 477785)*

❖

OPEN: all year, Mon–Sat, 10.00am–5.00pm,
Sun 11.00am–5.00pm

BUILDINGS OF BATH MUSEUM
Countess of Huntingdon's Chapel,
The Paragon *(01225 333895)*
❖
OPEN: mid Feb–Nov, Tues–Sun and Bank Holiday Mon,
10.30am–5.00pm

SCHOOLHOUSE GALLERY,
The Paragon *(01225 317707)*
❖
OPEN: mid Feb–Nov, Tues–Sun and Bank Holiday Mon,
10.30am–5.00pm

POSTAL MUSEUM,
Shire's Yard, 8 Broad Street *(01225 460333)*
❖
OPEN: all year, Mon–Sat, 11.00am–5.00pm,
Sun 2.00–5.00pm

ROYAL PHOTOGRAPHIC SOCIETY GALLERY,
The Octagon, Milsom Street (01225 462841)
❖
OPEN: all year, daily, 9.30am–5.30pm

GUILDHALL,
High Street *(01225 477785)*
❖
OPEN: all year, Mon–Fri, 9.00am–5.00pm

VICTORIA ART GALLERY,
Bridge Street *(01225 477785)*
❖
OPEN: all year, Mon–Fri, 10.00am–5.30pm,
Sat 10.00am–5.00pm

HOLBURNE MUSEUM,
Great Pulteney Street *(01225 466669)*
❖
OPEN: Easter–mid Nov, Mon–Sat, 11.00am–5.00pm,
Sun, 2.30–5.30pm;
mid Feb–Easter, mid Nov–mid Dec,
Tues–Sat, 11.00am–5.00pm, Sun, 2.30–5.30pm

SALLY LUNN'S,
4 North Parade Passage *(01225 461634)*

❖

Museum: open all year, Mon–Sat, 10.00am–6.00pm,
Sun 12.00am–6.00pm;
Tea Shop: open all year, Mon–Sat, 10.00am–11.00pm,
Sun, 12.00am–11.00pm

AMERICAN MUSEUM,
Claverton Manor, Claverton *(01225 460503)*

❖

OPEN: mid March–Nov, Tues–Sun, 2.00–5.00pm

BECKFORD'S TOWER,
Lansdown *(01225 338727)*
OPEN: March–Oct, Sat, Sun and Bank Holiday Mon,
2.00–5.00pm

BOOK MUSEUM,
Manvers Street *(01225 466000)*

❖

OPEN: all year, Mon–Fri, 9.00am–5.30pm,
Sat, 9.30am–1.00pm

WILLIAM HERSCHEL MUSEUM,
19 New King Street *(01225 311342)*

❖

OPEN: March–Oct, daily, 2.00–5.00pm;
Nov–Feb, Sat and Sun. 2.00–5.00pm

MR BOWLER'S BUSINESS (Bath Industrial
Heritage Centre), Julian Road *(01225 318348)*

❖

OPEN: Easter–Oct, daily, 10.00am–4.30pm;
Nov–Easter Sat and Sun, 10.00am–4.30pm

PRIOR PARK (National Trust),
Ralph Allen Drive

❖

OPEN: all year, Wed–Mon, 12.00am–5.30pm or dusk
telephone *01985 843600* for information; disabled visitors
should ring *01225 833422* to reserve one of the three
available parking bays; other visitors must arrive by bus,
taxi or bicycle; there is no parking available

Tourist Offices

Most of the Cotswolds lie within the 'Heart of England' the main office for which is at:

> The Heart of England Tourist Board, Larkhill Road, Worcester WR5 2EW [01905 763436]

Other offices are listed below; those open all year are indicated by [A] and those open only in the summer by [S]:

Bath [A]
Abbey Chambers, Abbey Churchyard, Bath BA1 1LY [01225 477101]

Broadway [S]
1 Cotswold Court, The Green, Broadway WR12 7AA [01386 852937]

Burford [A]
The Brewery, Sheep Street, Burford OX18 4LP [01993 823558]

Cheltenham [A]
Municipal Offices, 77 The Promenade, Cheltenham GL50 1PP
[01242 522878]

Chipping Campden [S]
The Town Hall, Chipping Campden GL55 6AT [01386 841206]

Cirencester [A]
The Corn Hall, Market Place, Cirencester GL7 2NW [01285 654180]

Moreton-in-Marsh [S]
The Council Offices, High Street, Moreton-in-Marsh GL5 6OA
[01608 50881]

Northleach [S]
Cotswold Countryside Collection, Northleach GL54 3JH [01451 860715]

Painswick [S]
The Library, Stroud Road, Painswick GL6 6UT [01452 813552]

Stow-on-the-Wold [A]
Hollis House, The Square, Stow-on-the-Wold GL54 1AF
[01451 831082]

Stroud [A]
Subscription Rooms, George Street, Stroud GL5 1AE
[01453 765768]

Tetbury [S]
The Old Court House, Tetbury GL8 8AA [01666 503552]

Winchcombe [S]
The Town Hall, High Street, Winchcombe GL54 5LJ [01684 594200]

Woodstock [A]
Hensington Road, Woodstock OX20 1JQ [011905 726311]

Town Data

The main centres for the Cotswolds are:

Bath: population: 85,000; the city lies close to the M4 motorway (which passes to the north) and a few miles west of the M5. There is a bus station, to the south of the Abbey, with connections to all of Britain's major cities. Close to the bus station is the railway station. Bath lies on the GWR line which runs from Bristol and the south-west to London.

Cheltenham: population: 107,000; the city lies close to the M5 motorway (which passes a short distance to the west) and is connected by a dual carriageway (A417/A419 – nearing completion at the time of writing) to the M4 at Swindon. There is a bus station close to the Promenade with connections to London and other major cities. The railway station lies to the west of the town centre. From it trains depart northwards to Worcester and Birmingham, and south to Gloucester, with onward connections to London and Bristol and the south-west.

Cirencester: population: 19,500; the new A417/A419 connects the town to the M4 at Swindon and the M5 at Gloucester/Cheltenham. There is no bus station, but coaches en route from Cheltenham/Gloucester to London stop at the eastern end of the town. There are also regular connections to Cheltenham for onward journeys to northern cities and to Bristol for journeys to the south-west. There is no railway station at Cirencester.

For the sites given below 'specified times' means that the site is open only at specific times of the day or of the year. These are as indicated at the end of each chapter. The indication 'any time' means that access is unrestricted.

Antiques

The Cotswolds have the largest number of antique dealers outside London. They may be found throughout the area, but chiefly in Bath, Broadway, Burford, Cheltenham, Cirencester and Stow-on-the Wold.

FACTFILE

Arts and Crafts

All sites at specified times

Bath
Hot Bath Gallery, Hotbath Street
Museum of East Asian Art
Royal Photographic Society Gallery
Schoolhouse Gallery, The Paragon
Victoria Art Gallery

Beckford
Beckford Silk

Bourton-on-the-Water
Cotswold Perfumery, Victoria Street
Bourton Pottery , Clapton Row

Cheltenham
Town Museum and Art Gallery

Chipping Campden
D.T. Hart (silversmith); Diane Hassall (shoes); Neil Jordan (silver
jewellery), The Silk Mill, Sheep Street
Robert Welch (silverware and cutlery), Lower High Street
Ann Smith (jewellery and enamel), Peacock House
Martin Gotrel (jewellery), The Square

Chipping Norton
Oxfordshire Craft Guild Shop, 7 Goddards Lane

Cirencester
Brewery Arts, Brewery Court

Conderton
Elaine Rippon Hand-painted Silk Studio, Darkes House
Toff Milway's, Conderton Pottery, The Old Forge

Filkins
Cotswold Woollen Weavers
Filkins Gallery and Studio, Cross Tree

Moreton-in-Marsh
Wellington Aviation Museum and Art Gallery, Broadway Road

Painswick
Painswick Woodcrafts (Dennis French), New Street

Stroud
Rooksmoor Mill, on the A46 south of Stroud

Cinemas and Theatres

There are cinemas in Bath, Cheltenham, Cirencester and Dursley, and also in Bristol, Gloucester, Oxford and Swindon which lie just outside the AONB. There are theatres in Bath, Cheltenham, Cirencester, Stroud, and also at Bristol, Oxford and Gloucester.

Gardens and Parks

All sites at specified times

Barnsley
Barnsley House Gardens

Bath
Dyrham Park [National Trust], to the north of the city
Prior Park [National Trust], Ralph Allen Drive

Bourton-on-the-Hill
Batsford Park Arboretum

Broadway
Broadway Tower Country Park, Fish Hill

Kemerton
The Priory

Mickleton
Kiftsgate Court Garden, Mickleton
Hidcote Manor Garden [National Trust], Hidcote Bartrim

Miserden
Misarden Park Gardens

North Cerney
Cerney House Gardens

Shipton Moyne
Hodges Barn Gardens

Tetbury
Westonbirt Arboretum

Winchcombe
Sudeley Castle and Gardens

Painswick
Rococo Garden, Painswick House

Woodstock
Blenheim Palace

Historical Sites

Open at specified times unless otherwise stated

Archaeological Sites
Cheltenham
Crickley Hill Iron Age Hillfort, any time

Hawkesbury Upton
Nan Tow's Tump (Bronze Age Round Barrow), any time

Little Sodbury
Little Sodbury Iron Age Hillfort, any time

Long Compton
Rollright Stones (Neolithic/
Bronze Age sites), any time

Notgrove
Notgrove Neolithic Long Barrow
[English Heritage], any time

Nympsfield
Nympsfield Neolithic Long
Barrow [English Heritage],
Coaley Peak Picnic Site, any
time

Uley
Uley Tumulus (Hetty Pegler's
Tump) Neolithic Long Barrow,
any time
Uleybury Iron Age Hillfort, any
time

Winchcombe
Belas Knap Neolithic Long
Barrow [English Heritage], any
time

Historical Buildings
Bath
Assembly Rooms
Beckford's Tower
Dyrham Park [National Trust]
(north of the city)
Guildhall
No.1 Royal Crescent
Pump Room
Sally Lunn's

Bibury
Arlington Mill (Museum)

Bourton-on-the-Hill
Sezincote House

Cheltenham
Cheltenham College
Pittville Pump Room

Cirencester
Town Lock-Up

Combe
Combe Saw Mill

Edge Hill
Upton House [National Trust]

Horton
Horton Court [National Trust]

Lower Slaughter
The Old Mill

Moreton-in-Marsh
Chastleton House [National
Trust]

Northleach
Cotswold Countryside Collection
(Old County Gaol)

Nympsfield
Woodchester Mansion

Painswick
Prinknash Abbey

Snowshill
Snowshill Manor

Stanway
Stanway House

Tetbury
Chavenage House
Westonbirt House

Uley
Owlpen Manor

Whittington
Whittington Court

Winchcombe
Sudeley Castle

Woodstock
Blenheim Palace

Medieval Sites
Bredon
Tithe Barn [National Trust]

Winchcombe
Hailes Abbey

Roman/Saxon Sites
Bath
Roman baths

Chipping Campden
Kiftsgate Stone, any time

Cirencester
Roman amphitheatre and town
   wall, any time

Great Witcombe
Roman villa
exterior may be seen at any
   time; guided tours at specified
   times

Yanworth
Chedworth Roman Villa [National
   Trust]

Hotels and Restaurants

As a major tourist area the Cotswolds has a superb range of accommodation and restaurants from which the visitor may chose. The choice is assisted by Where to Stay in The Heart of England, available from the Heart of England Tourist Board's main office, and from local lists at the larger Tourist Information Offices. Of the latter, the best guides are The Cotswolds Accommodation Guide, jointly produced by Cotswold West Oxfordshire District Councils; The Undiscovered Cotswolds, an accommodation list produced by Stroud District Council; and Where to Stay, What to Visit, Where to Eat and Where to Shop, produced by the Bath Tourism Bureau. These are available from the local Tourist Information Offices.

   A sample of hotels and restaurants in or near the three main tourist centres (Bath, Cheltenham and Cirencester) appears below. The lists have been derived from personal experience or recommendation, but the author and publisher cannot be held responsible if your visit does not match your expectations. A simple price guide – £ = inexpensive, ££ = moderate, £££ = expensive – is given as a help.

Hotels
Bath
The Royal Crescent Hotel, Royal Crescent, Bath [01225 739955]
de luxe hotel in the one of Britain's great streets [£££]

The Priory Hotel, Weston Road, Bath [01225 331922]
lovely country house with beautiful gardens [£££]

Dukes Hotel, Great Pulteney Street, Bath [01225 463512]
Grade I listed Georgian town house close to city centre [££]

Pratt's Hotel, South Parade, Bath [01225 460441]
elegant town house close to city centre; good restaurant [££]

The Old Schoolhouse, Church Street, Bathford [01225 859593]
converted schoolhouse in 'village' close to Bath [£]

Barrow Castle, Rush Hill, Bath [01225 480725]
unusual Victorian castle; lovely peaceful gardens [£]

Cheltenham
Queen's Hotel, The Promenade, Cheltenham [01242 514724]
wonderfully elegant and close to town centre [£££]

Lord of the Manor Hotel, Upper Slaughter [01451 820243]
fabulous old manor house [£££]

The Cotswold Grange Hotel, Pittville Circus Road, Cheltenham
[01242 515119] fine house some away from town centre,
but near Pittville Park [££]

The Frogmill Hotel, Shipton Oliffe [01242 820547]
lovely old building well situated for touring; a car is essential [££]

Cleeve Hill Hotel, Cleeve Hill, Cheltenham [01242 672052]
charming; fine views; no restaurant [£]

The Old New Inn, Bourton-on-the-Water [01451 820467]
at the heart of the village [£]

Cirencester
Stratton House Hotel, Gloucester Road, Cirencester [01285 651761]
lovely, creeper-clad hotel; well-situated for exploring [£££]
The Hare and Hounds Hotel, Westonbirt [01666 880233]
fine old country hotel [£££]

Raydon House Hotel, 3 The Avenue, Cirencester [01285 653485]
Victorian house close to town centre [££]

Bibury Court Hotel, Bibury [01285 740337]
ivy-clad coaching inn on the river [££]

Dix's Barn, Duntisbourne Abbots [01285 821249]
converted barn; small, with limited facilities; very quiet and pleasant [£]

Royal Agricultural College, Cirencester [01285 652531]
very reasonable accommodation in an unexpected place [££]

Restaurants

Bath

Milburns, The Pump Room, Stall Street, Bath [01225 444477]
the height of elegance [£££]

Popjoys, Beau Nash House, Saw Close, Bath [01225 460494]
good food in one of Bath's most historic houses [££]

Sally Lunn's, North Parade Passage, Bath [01225 461634]
good food in the oldest house in Bath [£]

Cheltenham

Number Twelve, 12 Suffolk Parade, Cheltenham [01242 584544]
in the heart of the town's antique quarter [££]

Below Stairs, 103 The Promenade, Cheltenham [01242 234599]
wonderful food close to the centre of town [££]

Eleven North Place, 11 North Place, Cheltenham [01242 250343]
good basic menu [£]

Cirencester

Harry Hare's, 3 Gosditch Street, Cirencester [01285 652375]
marvellous old building and great food [£££]

Gianni's, 30 Castle Street, Cirencester [01285 643133]
best Italian restaurant in the area [££]

Bathurst Arms, North Cerney [01285 831281]
beautiful position beside the river; local produce on the menu [££]

Leisure Activities

Gliding

Gliding taster flights and courses are available at the Bristol and Gloucestershire Gliding Club at Frocester Hill, Nympsfield, near Stonehouse [01453 860342]

Golf

Bath

Bath Golf Club, Sham Castle [01225 425182/463834]
Lansdown Golf Club, Lansdown [01225 422138/425007]

Broadway

Broadway Golf Course, Willersley Hill [01386 853683]

Burford

Burford Golf Club [01993 822149]

Cirencester
Cirencester Golf Course, Bagendon [01285 653939]

Cheltenham
Cleeve Hill Golf Course, Cleeve Hill [01242 672025]
Cotswold Hills Golf Course, Ullenwood [01242 515264]
Lilley Brook Golf Course, Charlton Kings [01242 580715]

Minchinhampton
Minchinhampton Old Course [01453 832642]
Minchinhampton New Course [01453 833866]

Naunton
Naunton Downs Golf Course, Stow Road [01451 850090]

Painswick
Painswick Golf Course [01452 812180]

Stinchcombe
Stinchcombe Hill Golf Course, Stinchcombe Hill, near Dursley
[01453 542015]

Wotton-under-Edge
Cotswold Edge Golf Club, Wotton-under-Edge [01453 844167]

Horse Riding

The Cotswolds has numerous bridleways and riding centres: ask at
the local Tourist Information Centres for details. There is also horse
racing at Bath and Cheltenham, the latter including the famous Gold
Cup meeting in March; the Badminton Three-Day Event in April, and
an annual event at Gatcombe Park in August. There is a regular
programme of polo matches at Cirencester Park during the summer.

Motor Sports

There is a regular programme of events for both motor cycles and
cars at the Castle Combe racing circuit. Hill climbs are held about
three times each year at Prescott, near Cheltenham.

Sports Centres

There are sports centres at Bath, Cheltenham, Cirencester and
Stroud, as well as at Bristol and Gloucester.

Swimming Pools

There are swimming pools at Bath, Cheltenham, Cirencester, Stroud
and Wotton-under-Edge, as well as the nearby cities of Bristol and
Gloucester.

Walking

The Cotswolds provide an excellent area for walking, most of the country being flat or gently sloping (apart from the Cotswold Edge and one or two of the steeper valleys, though even here the climbing is limited). The Tourist Information Centres have details of local walks, some of which are guided. There are also a number of small publications on walking in the area. The Cotswold Way is a 100-mile route following the Cotswold edge from Chipping Campden to Bath. At present it is maintained by the county councils and voluntary groups, but it is planned to become a National Trail.

Water Sports

All forms of water sports are available at the Cotswold Water Park, South Cerney.

Museums

All specified times

Agricultural

Northleach
Cotswold Countryside Collection

Historical

Bath
Book Museum
Buildings of Bath Museum
Heritage Vaults
Mr Bowler's Business (Bath
   Industrial Heritage Centre)
No.1 Royal Crescent (Georgian)
Postal Museum
Roman Baths
Sally Lunn's

Bibury
Arlington Mill Museum

Cirencester
Corinium Museum (Roman)

Wotton-under-Edge
Heritage Centre

Individuals

Bath
William Herschel Museum

Cheltenham
Holst Birthplace Museum

Military

Moreton-in-Marsh
Wellington Aviation Museum

Musical

Northleach
Keith Harding's World of
   Mechanical Music

Police

Northleach
Cotswold Countryside Collection

Tetbury
Police Bygones Museum

Winchcombe
Folk and Police Museum

Sporting
Cheltenham
Hall of Fame, Cheltenham
    Racecourse

Town and General Museums
Bath
American Museum
Buildings of Bath Museum
Museum of Costume/Fashion
    Research Centre
Museum of East Asian Art

Burford
Tolsey Museum

Cheltenham
Town Museum
Pittville Pump Room Museum

Chipping Norton
Museum of Local History

Lower Slaughter
The Old Mill

Winchcombe
Folk and Police Museum

Toys
Bourton-on-the-Water
Cotswolds Motor Museum and
    Toy Collection

Broadway
Teddy Bear Museum

Transport
Bourton-on-the-Water
Cotswolds Motor Museum and
    Toy Collection

Cheltenham
The Bugatti Trust, Gotherington
    (north-east of the town)

Winchcombe
Railway Museum
Gloucestershire–Warwickshire
    Railway, Toddington (north of
    the town)

Other Visitor Sites

All at specified times

Bourton-on-the-Water
Model Railway Exhibition
Model Village
The Dragonfly Maze

Little Witcombe
Crickley Windward Vineyard

Northleach
The Dolls House

Winchcombe
Gloucestershire–Warwickshire
    Railway, Toddington
North Gloucestershire Railway,
    Toddington

Picnic Sites

All sites open at any time

Andoversford
Kilkenny Viewpoint

Tormarton
Tog Hill

Nympsfield
Coaley Peak

Wildlife

All sites at specified times

Bibury
Bibury Trout Farm

Blockley
Sleepy Hollow Farm Park,
   Draycott Road

Bourton-on-the-Water
Cotswold Falconry Centre,
   Batsford Park
Birdland, Rissington Road

Burford
Cotswold Wildlife Park

Condicote
Donnington Trout Farm

Notgrove
Folly Farm

Painswick
Prinknash Bird Park

Temple Guiting
Cotswold Farm Park

Index